AN JOAN THE CRONE

The History And Craft
Of The Cornish Witch

Kelvin I. Jones

OAKMAGIC PUBLICATIONS 1999

AN JOAN THE CRONE

The History And Craft
Of The Cornish Witch

Kelvin. I. Jones

ISBN: 1 901163 93 8

First published by
OAKMAGIC BOOKS

1999

Illustrations: C. The Author.

Sections of this book previously appeared
as "Seven Cornish Witches" and "Cornish
Witchcraft" (now unavailable).

For a complete list of over 80
titles on all aspects of Cornish
folklore, antiquities etc., send
SAE to the publisher at this
address:

OAKMAGIC PUBLICATIONS,
2 SOUTH PLACE FOLLY,
PENZANCE TR18 4JB.

Also available from the same publisher:
Witchcraft In Cornwall (£2.50)
Cornish Charms And Cures (£2.50)

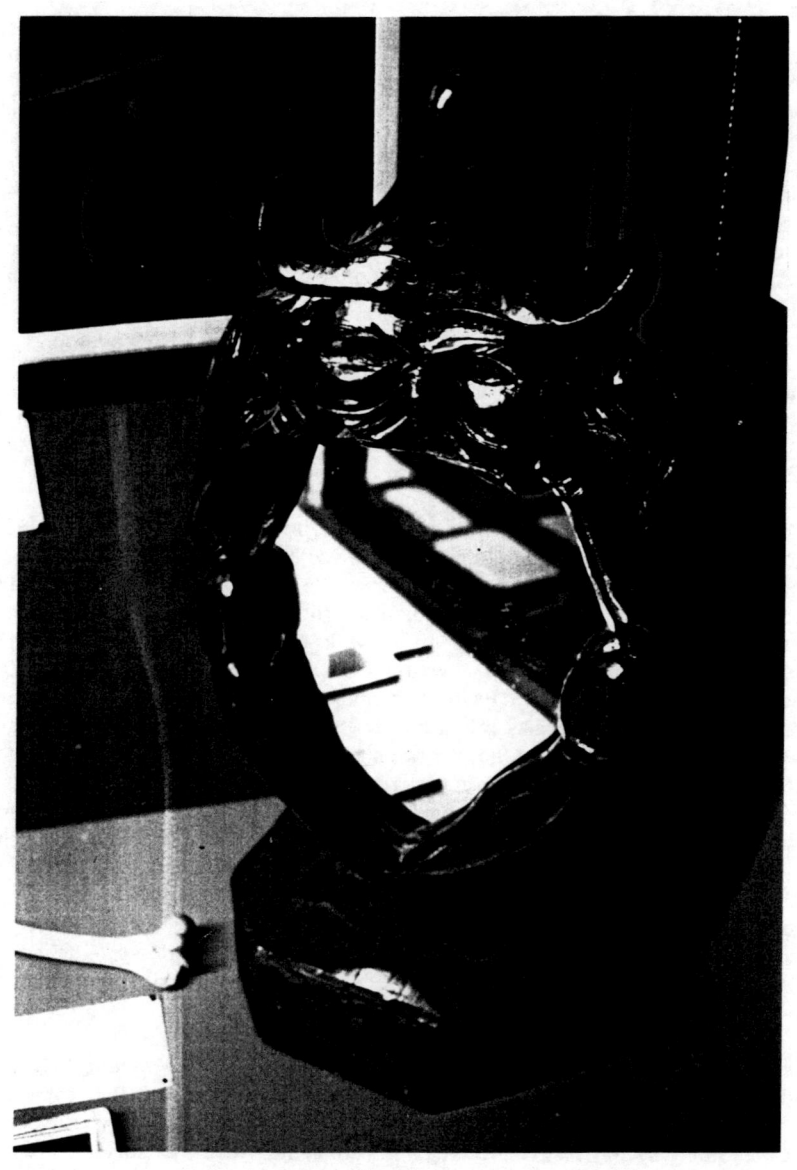

Unusual scrying mirror. From the Museum of Witchcraft. Photo: The author, courtesy: Graham King.

INTRODUCTION

The history of witchcraft in Cornwall is as much a matter of perception and conjecture as is the broad history of witchcraft itself. There is much evidence to suggest that not only did witchcraft exist as a living tradition and practice within this remote area but that it did so until a comparatively late period. Today it is all but extinct and is only truly represented by the activities of modern day pagans who provide themselves with the title of "witches". We must be careful here, however, for the modern witch is as chalk and cheese to the traditional proponent of that tradition. The ideas fostered by Gerald Gardner and others have very little to do with the traditional witch and are largely a reinvention of 19th Century magical traditions, despite their protestations to the contrary.

The purpose of this volume is to bring to light the hidden corners of traditional witchcraft in Cornwall, whether by referring to historical "fact", opinion, myth or folklore. Cornwall, because of its isolated position, retains much of this, though it has to be said that serious historians have never bothered much with the subject, considering it, I suspect, of little importance to them.

There have been only two figures of significance, to my knowledge, in the field of study represented by this book. One is Cecil Williamson, the former curator and owner of the Museum of Witchcraft at Boscastle and the other William Paynter, formerly of St Ives. Neither of these scholars sought fit to publish very much, and that is very much a disappointment for those with an interest in the subject. Cecil Williamson is unlikely to divulge the fruits of his many years' labour as I write because of illness and William Paynter is no longer with us. Both men possessed extensive collections of artefacts relating to the subject which would certainly interest the world at large. Both might have written books on the subject but did not. The former retained an enormous amount of research material which fortunately is now available to researchers under the aegis of the new owner, Graham King. An avid collector, Cecil overlooked very little in his desire to collect evidence of witchcraft from the far corners of the West Country and in completing this volume, I often found myself following in his erudite footsteps. Of the enigmatic William Paynter, once recorder of the Callington Old Cornwall Society, I have less to say, except that I wished I might have met him. He lived in a time when attitudes to witchcraft and belief in its undoubted power were still in evidence, in an age prior to television and late twentieth century scepticisim.

This book is for them and for all those who have aided me on my quest. It aims to provide a complete guide to the subject and if my readers object that some of the material has appeared elsewhere before now, I would answer that the subject is an ever expanding one as fresh material comes to light. Much has survived, especially from the last century and there is probably more waiting to be teased out of newspapers and the bowels of record offices even as I write this.

Much of the early history of this subject about which so much has been written but so little understood has not survived except for a passing reference or two in a gaol book. Cornwall was not as fortunate as Devon, its neighbouring county, in retaining records of witchcraft accusations and trials during the heyday of the persecutions of the 17th Century. This period is therefore somewhat under represented and hazy. From what we know of the period (and it is a late period at that), the judiciary were extremely lenient with cases that came before them on the Western Assize circuit, being only too ready to dismiss the accusations out of hand, rather than pursue them. The same was true also, to a lesser extent in Devonshire. What do survive from this period are the possession cases like that of the Tonken affair and also the case of Anne Jefferies, where it is difficult to separate genuine ideas about witchcraft from political conspiracy. In fact, as several modern investigators of witchcraft have shown, it is fallacious even to separate witchcraft from the social milieu which encompassed it during that period of unrest and upheaval. The same was true in Cornwall as anywhere else in Britain.

What also rings loud and clear throughout all the accounts in this book is the absolute conviction both in the idea that one could be ill-wished or rendered harm by witchcraft and that witches had great power to curse or heal. By the nineteenth century the idea of the "white witch" had taken prominence. The emphasis was on removing curses or ill luck at all costs and this obsession led to the amassed fortunes of women like Tamsin Blight. This belief did not arise from empty space: it was rooted in centuries of belief and evidence. Tamsin Blight herself is a useful yardstick, for there are accounts of her ability to conjure spirits, remove and place curses, thus proving that she enjoyed a credibility in both her light and dark aspects. What this guide also demonstrates to the reader is the absolute fiction of the idea of witches' covens and the notion that in some way witchcraft was part of an organised religious belief system. Such ideas cannot be proved, certainly not within Cornwall, and must remain the province of Dr Murray and certain members of the Christian community. The fact that some modern witches encourage such notions does not help the job of the folklorist and historian. Where I have therefore referred in the text to "the old religion" I mean simply a set of beliefs which were grounded in everyday practice, much of it handed down through generations.

Kelvin I. Jones

Penzance, November 1999.

Part One:
Lives Of The Cornish Witches

The accounts of the women chronicled in this section of the book reveal a great deal of common ground. Each of the women described existed on the edge of society. Some would have been uneasy with the term witch, for the very word was a kind of anathema in Cornish society of the time. Moreover, the word certainly did not describe, as it does in modern paganism, a set of recognised beliefs and methods. Some of the subjects, like Anne Jefferies, were referred to by their accusers as witches but stolidly maintained their belief in Christianity. Indeed, this was often the case during the earlier witch trials. The spells and charms they may have used were overtly Christian in their imagery and would have been well known in the folk consciousness of the period. The subjects described here were, like many women who are referred to in the trial material of earlier periods, quite secretive in their dealings, the only exception being, perhaps, Tamsin Blight. Some were referred to by their contemporaries as "white witches", an appellation which has caused scholars and historians a deal of confusion. The term itself originates from a time when, at a folk level, it was thought possible to remove a curse or effect of ill-wishing upon the victim. In Cornwall the term "pellar" was often used, meaning "repeller" of curses or ill wishes. This was usually an occupation which originated from a conferred gift (as in the case of the pellar of Cury) and which was often handed down through generations. Many pellars were male, although Blight, who was also described as a "witch" is elsewhere referred to as a "pellar" in the literature of the time.

Another factor which unites these women was their age and maturity. There are a number of examples of young women arraigned of the crime of maleficia but no real evidence of this in Cornwall. Above all, one common thread runs through them all: they operated (sometimes quite successfully) on the margins of society and were often surprisingly successful in supplementing their income through practising the arts of divination, herbal cures and, to some degree, necromancy. The cumulative evidence presented here to the reader suggests that witchcraft, as it was known to people in Cornwall prior to the modern period, was not an organized or recognisable religion, as was once thought to be the case, but more a set of perceptions and beliefs in the folk mind. This in turn was based deeply in the wider understanding of the way in which Mankind related to Nature. The power of a curse to harm should not be underestimated when reading these accounts and the fear of the witch was paramount. Condemnation of witchcraft, although supported by the Church, was not originated by that body and the real accusers of the witch were the ordinary people themselves. Sometimes, of course, witchcraft was used as a method in order to stifle genuine political or religious contention, as in the case of Anne Jefferies. Lastly, the evidence from newspapers of the period 1750 - 1900 suggests that most people in Cornwall not only understood very well what witchcraft was but they most certainly knew of a witch, either from first or second hand experience and possibly anecdote.

TAMSIN BLIGHT

Tamsin Blight, or "Tammy Blee", as she was otherwise known by her contemporaries, was perhaps the most well known and most widely documented of the witches of Cornwall. Although she is referred to by the folklorist, William Bottrell, as a witch, she also goes under the name of "pellar" ("the pellar of Helston"), the term pellar meaning one who repelled spells or charms. Her reputation was an entirely benevolent one and she appear to have healed and cured hundreds of people in the Helston area and further west to as far as the Land's End District from where people would bring their loved ones miles on stretchers to visit her and obtain a cure.

Tammy was born in Redruth in 1798 and local tradition has it that she could claim to be a direct descendant of true pellar blood. Her name is sometimes spelt "Blee", which is a common Cornish word meaning "wolf". Her Christian name is also sometimes spelt by her contemporaries as "Tamson". Although we know virtually nothing of her early life, we find that she married a widower called James (or Jemmy) Thomas in 1835 when she was already thirty eight. As a single woman plying her craft of curing and conjuring, she may have already built up a reputation by this time and been grateful for the protection a male companion may have offered her. Even at this relatively late period in the history of witchcraft it was still unsafe to practise the craft of witch as a single woman. As late as the mid nineteenth century there are accounts in newspapers of pellars or cunning men being attacked because fellow villagers feared their power or reputations. It is conceivable that Tammy herself was relatively poor, for one account of her collected by W.H. Paynter in the 1920's records that as a child the correspondent "used to be put to bed with her," a common practice amongst the lower classes at this time.

James Thomas would have given Tammy the added financial security she might have enjoyed. Few pellars relied solely on their craft as their main source of income, although in Tammy's case she did very well out of it. As for Thomas, he also claimed to possess occult powers. A story connected with that time of her life after she had married concerns Jemmy and would indicate that for some while before she went to live in Helston she lodged near Illogan with her husband.

It appears that Tammy was in the habit of picking "cherks" or half burnt cinders from a pile of ashes which were kept outside the boiler house where Jemmy worked. On one occasion she was spoken to in derisory fashion by one of the captains who accused her of having stolen some pieces of timber which had gone missing from the mine. Little more was said, but the following day, when the men came to start the pumping engine, which had been stopped in order to carry out routine repairs, they found that the engine would not start. The mine had started very quickly to fill up with water and the matter was a serious one. The captain put two and two together and, suspecting that someone may have put a spell on the machinery, he sent for Tammy. Tammy arrived at the mine, and with great relish, removed the spell, having been paid handsomely for her skills.

Later in her life, as has been already mentioned, Tammy moved to Helston and it was there that she and Jemmy were most successful. However, it seems likely that eventually Thomas separated from Tammy. Contemporary reports indicate that it was Tammy who was the stronger of the partners and that her husband earned an unsavoury reputation. Although one account tells us that Jemmy "was endowed with similar occult powers," another says that he tried unsuccessfully to earn a living for himself as a "conjuror" (this was another loose term applied to pellars or white witches and was usually applied to those who had some book knowledge of so called "high magic". Many of the pellars and cunning men and women had a magical book which they obtained either through mail order or through one of their ancestors, containing spells and magical formulae.)

A third account links Tammy to the famous Matthew Lutey of Cury who, according to the famous Cornish legend, enshrined by William Bottrell, released a mermaid into the sea and was thereafterwards blessed with the gift of the pellar for generations to come. The account goes on to describe how:

"... there are hundreds alive to testify among those who yearly consult Tammy Blee and J Thomas. This worthy couple of white witches seem to be equally successful in the exercise of their art, though many say that the former only is of the true old peller blood."

Jemmy did much to harm Tammy's own genuine reputation as a pellar and to the pellar reputation was often critical since you not only had to be seen to be effective but you also had to be seen to be straight in your dealings.

Jemmy's outrageous conduct was reported widely in the pages of the West Briton newspaper of the time and later reprinted by Robert Hunt, that indefatigable folklore collector of the late 19th Century. Hunt quotes once account in which Jemmy used his influence to seduce a tradesman and a sea captain. According to the West Briton,

"During the week ending Sunday last, a "wise man" from Illogan has been engaged with about half a dozen witchcraft cases, one a young tradesman and another a sea-captain. It appears that the "wise man" was in the first place visited at his home by these deluded people at different times, and he declared the whole of them to be spell-bound. In one case he said that if the person had not come so soon, in about a fortnight he would have been in the asylum; another would have had his leg broken; and in every case something direful would have happened. Numerous incantations have been performed. In the case of a captain of a vessel, a visit was paid to the seaside, and while the "wise man" uttered some unintelligible gibberish, the captain had to throw a stone into the sea. So heavy was the spell under which he laboured, and which immediately fell back upon the "wise man", that the latter pretended that he could scarcely walk back to Hayle. The most abominable part of the incantation is performed during the hours of midnight, and for that purpose the wretch sleeps with his victims, and for five nights following he had five different bed-fellows. Having no doubt repaid a pretty good harvest during the week, he returned to his home on Monday; but such was the pretended effect produced by the different spells and witchcraft that tell upon him from his many dupes, that two of the young men who had been under his charge were obliged to obtain a horse and cart and carry him to the Hayle Station. One of the men, having had two "spells" resting on him, the "wise man" was obliged to sleep with him on Saturday and Sunday nights, having spent the whole of Sunday in his diabolical work."

The article solemnly concludes with these words:

"It is time that the police, or some other higher authorities, should take the matter up, as the person alluded to is well known, and frequently visited by the ignorant and superstitious."

Even though the reporter's homophobia is evident in this article, it is clear that Jemmy was preying upon the gullible to satisfy his own lusts. And despite the newspaper "revelations", he did not stop his dubious career as a spell remover and seducer of men. Under a subsequent headline of "Gross Superstition At Hayle", we find this article:

"A correspondent has furnished us with the following particulars relative to the antecedents of the pretended conjurer. He states that James Thomas, the conjurer from the parish of Illogan, married some time since the late celebrated Tammy Blee of Redruth, who afterwards removed to Helston and carried on as a fortune teller, but parted from her husband, James Thomas, on account of a warrant for his apprehension having been issued against him by the magistrates of St Ives, for attempting to take a spell from Mrs Paynter, through her husband, William Paynter, who stated before the magistrates that he wanted to commit a disgraceful offence. (A euphemism for homosexual favours - KJ) Thomas then absconded, and was absent from the West of Cornwall for upwards of two years. His wife then stated that the virtue was in her and not in him; that she was of the real "Pellar" blood; and that he could tell nothing but through her. His greatest dupes have been at St Just and Hayle, and other parts of the west of Cornwall. He has been in the habit of receiving money annually for keeping witchcraft from vessels sailing out of Hayle. He slept with several of his dupes recently; and about a fortnight since he stated that he must sleep with certain young men at Copperhouse, Hayle, in order to protect them from something that was hanging over them, one of them being a mason and the other a miner, the two latter lately from St Just. He said himself this week at Truro that he had cured a young man from St Erth, and was going on Saturday again to take a spell from the father, a tin smelter. He has caused a great disturbance amongst the neighbours, by charging some with having bewitched others. He is a drunken, disgraceful, beastly fellow, and ought to be sent to the treadmill. One of the young men is thoroughly ashamed of himself to think he has been duped so by this scoundrel."

We hear little more of Jemmy until the 26th of February, 1874 when, under the headline, "Death of A Wizard", we discover the following obituary in the West Briton:

On Thursday last, at Park bottom, in the parish of Illogan, John Thomas, better known as "the wizard", ended his mortal career...Rich and poor for miles around have honoured him with a visit(in times past) and the contributions poured in upon him must, if report be true, have been considerable. Every species of ailment which afflicts the human family he was supposed to cure. If swine were possessed of unnatural propensities, or took to dying in an unceremonious manner, John could tell their owners all about it; or if cows misbehaved themselves, adopted vicious tricks and refused to do the correct thing, the wizard soon brought them to their senses. Among horses he was indeed a host; a kicker might as well be a dead horse, as far as kicking went, after John had worked his will on him: and as to stopping blood, if an arm was lopped off no blood would flow if John cried stop..."

Obviously, over the years since his wife Tammy's death in 1856, Jemmy's reputation had improved. At his wife's death his occupation is registered as "copper miner" and there is a clue here that he may have lost his previous, more lucrative job because of the publicity he had received concerning his homosexual romps.

Although Tammy died many years before her husband, once in Helston her own reputation began to prosper. According to William Bottrell, who collected some of the stories about Tammy and her husband almost at first hand, the spring was the busiest period for the little house in Meneage Street where Tammy set up her Pellar's practice. People would visit in the spring to have their amulets, charms or spells renewed, for "it is believed that when the sun is returning, the Pellar has more power to protect them from bad luck than at any other season."

Of course, Tammy and her husband were not the only pellars in the area. In the neighbouring town to Jemmy's Redruth lived another wise woman whose renown for effecting cures was such that people were often brought to her from places as far away as the Lizard. According to Hamilton Jenkin (Cornwall And Its People, Dent, 1945): "A few years since, the writer was informed that a woman who is still living in the district had been cured by this witch of a haemorrhage, when lying almost at death's door. It appears that the only advice given her was to drink warm beer, but so efficacious did this prove that she rapidly recovered and has never known any return of the affliction to this day."

According to Bottrell, the journeys undertaken by Tammy's clients were remarkable and long and her clientele consisted of people of all ages and conditions. There were people visiting her from the Scilly Isles, captains of vessels from Hayle, St Ives and even Swansea. Many seamen would undertake to have their charms renewed before undergoing a hazardous sea voyage.

In Bottrell's account of the Helston household he refers to the Pellar as "he", which is a little confusing. Can we assume that in the early days Jemmy was controlling the buisiness and that it was only in the later period that Tammy took over ? Quite possibly. At any rate, Bottrell gives us a vivid insight into the procedure used by the couple. Apparently there was a crowd waiting outside the Meneage Street house prior to the doors being opened and the clients being admitted. Then they would be invited in singly to the room "styled the hale(hall)." He then goes on to say that "few remained closeted with him more than half an hour, during which time some were provided with little bags of earth , teeth or bones taken from a grave. These precious relics were to be worn, suspended from the neck, for the prevention or cure of fits, and other mysterious complaints supposed to be brought on by witchcraft. Others were furnished with a scrap of parchment, on which was written the ABRACADABRA, or the following charm: - SATOR, AREPO, TENET, OPERA,

ROTAS. These charms were then enclosed in a paper, curiously folded like a valentine, sealed and suspended from the neck of the ill-wished, spell-bound, or otherwise ailing person. The last charm is regarded as an instrument of great power, because the magical words read backwards as forwards. A gritty substance called witch powders, that looked very much like pounded brick, was also given to those who required it." Bottrell then goes on to observe that "an aged crone of the pellar blood, mother or sister of the white witch in chief, received some of the women upstairs to cure such of the least difficult cases, as simple charming would effect; but the greatest part of them preferred the man, as his charms only were powerful enough to unbewitch them."

This last comment might suggest that the Meneage Street house accommodated not only Jemmy and Tammy but also another, older relative. However, it is also possible that by this time Tammy may have resumed her relationship with Jemmy for a while. That the male pellar referred to is most certainly Jemmy is confirmed when, at the end of the article, Bottrell writes that an acquaintance of his who had had a run of bad luck, decided to visit "the wise man J.T. at his abode in or around Helston.".

Bottrell then goes on to describe one of the written charms commonly used by the "Pellar of Helston" and adds that "the following is a literal copy":

"On one side of a bit of paper, about an inch and a half by one inch, NALGAH. Here follows a picture of what must have been the conjuror's own creation, as such an object was never seen by mortal eyes in the heavens above... The only object we can compare it to is a something which is a cross between a headless cherub and a spread-eagle. Underneath what might have been intended for angel or bird, there is an egg, on which the creature appears to be brooding. There is another egg at the extremity of one of the outstretched legs of the creature. This picture, which is the most singular part of the charm, can only be represented by the aid of the pencil. The word TETRAGRAMMATON, is under it. On the reverse, JEHOVAH. JAH. ELOHIM. SHADDAY. ADONAY. HAVE MERCY ON A POOR WOMAN. From the worn condition of the charm (which had been in use many years before it came into our hands) it is difficult to make out the writing," he concludes.

It is evident that Bottrell had been given a charm which itself the pellar had derived from one of the medieval grimoires of a cabbalistic volume, many of which were available by mail order from dealers in London and which the Blights were no doubt in possession of. Bottrell goes on to add that other clients of Tammy and Jemmy were supplied with "blood stones, milpreves or snake-stones... manufactured by the pellar family to be worn as amulets. The blue stone rings, in which some fancied they saw the figure of an adder, or when marked with yellow veins the pattern of a snake, were particularly prized, because it was believed that those who wore them were by that means safe from being harmed by any reptile of the serpent tribe, and that man or beast, bit and envenomed, being given some water to drink, wherein the stone had been infused, would perfectly recover of the poison."

Many of the stories which have survived about Tammy's undoubted powers were collected by William Paynter who, during the early part of this century collected a great number of accounts of Cornish witches and their practices from the lips of their clients. About 1895 a portrait of Tamsin was purchased at an auction in Penzance. Today the portrait is in the possession of the Truro Museum. Measuring about three feet by two feet, it shows a woman of advanced years wearing a shawl and bonnet. The eyes in the portrait suggest a woman of some intelligence. At the time of the sale there was some controversy as to the identity of the artist and it was suggested that it might have painted by John Opie, or his brother, Edward, who lived in Plymouth. The inscription under the portrait reads: "Tamson Blight, the Helston Witch." Paynter subsequently wrote an article for the Mercury (Western Morning News) about Tammy in which he related many of the tales about her (June 4, 1928).

The first story related by Paynter provides eviedence of how the "repeller" of spells worked and how deep seated was people's fear of witchcraft and especially the fear of ill wishing.. A woman living near Helston had a child who was affected with a mysterious illness. Although medical treatment had been tried this was to no avail. Because the child was thought to be "ill wished", therefore a visit was made to Tamsin. The mother demanded to know the name of the ill wisher but Tamsin refused to oblige. However, she was willing to describe her appearance and at once the woman recognised her. Some days later she met the woman who had ill wished her child and scratched her arm and drew blood from her. From that hour the child began to get well and was able to leave her bed. Another story related to Paynter is recorded as follows:

"My mother lived beside a woman who was very ill and none seemed to know what was the matter with her, except that she was supposed to be ill-wished. Two neighbours one morning left the sick woman in bed and visited the witch to enquire what was the matter with the unfortunate woman and if there was any hope of a recovery. "Give me sixpence," said Tamson, "and I will tell you all about it." "We have no money", replied one of the women. "Oh yes you have !" said the witch, "put your hand into your pocket" and on doing so the woman discovered a sixpence, which she had placed there some time ago and forgotten. It was given her to go to the Copperhouse Fair.

"Handing the coin to Tamson, the latter said, "Go home, my dears, your neighbour is alright, and by the time you reach home she will have baked a heavy cake for your tea." On their arrival, they stated, they found the sick woman in the kitchen and quite well, and cutting a heavy cake which she had made and baked during their absence."

Another of Paynter's tales concerned a woman living at Breage who suffered from a "severe sickness", and being unable to move her limbs, was compelled to lie in the same position day after day. A neighbour informed her that the reason for her sickness was most probably ill wishing and it was decided there and then that he would take her in his dog cart to see Tammy in Helston. After certain incantations had been used, Tamson informed the woman that as soon as she arrived home, the one who had ill wished her would come to the door and say: "Is my little black cat here ?" The homeward journey was continued and on reaching the house, an old woman hobbled in and asked if she had seen her little black cat. Whereupon the sick woman got up from her chair and taking two pitchers, went to the well and drew water much to the amazement of the preacher who departed most upset.

Another correspondent of over 80 who was acquainted with Tamson used to have her fortune told and even had her husband described to her before she met him. Her story is as follows:

"When I was a girl, my master suffered many losses, which he attributed to the malign influence of some evil-disposed person. Tamson's help was sought and she advised as follows: "Go home, catch the cock, put him under the brandis (an iron tripod in common use with fires on the hearth for supporting crock or kettle) and cover him over with a red cloth. Then call together all your friends and neighbours and give them plenty to eat, and before their departure let each one stroke the brandis and the cock will crow over the one who stole." Returning home, the farmer did as he was directed, and each one in turn was requested to go through the ordeal. Now it happened that one old woman present refused, but the farmer, not wishing to be outdone, forced her and immediately she neared the brandis the cock crew and she thereupon made a confession, in which she stated that she alone was responsible for the ill-luck he had had."

Tamson was also of great assistance to farmers in the district. A farmer who possessed many acres of land and was in many respects a sensible man, was greatly annoyed to find that his cattle were becoming diseased in the spring. Nothing could satisfy him but to assume that they were ill-wished and he resolved to find out the person who had cast the evil eye upon them. A sum was paid to Tamson who advised him to confine his cattle until the next moon was as old as the present one. This, she explained, tamed the devils within them and sent them to a far away place where she could lock them up forever. He did as commanded and the spell was removed. Tamson advised another farmer to go home and take the heart of one of the animals which had met with a mysterious disease and burn it with fire in one of his fields at midnight at the same time uttering some strange words which she gave him.

Tamson was not without her dark side, it appears, for in addition to the story about the engine house I related earlier, there is also the tale about her shoe maker. In this account a shoe maker living in Camborne refused to mend her shoes because she was such a bad payer. In future, he told her, she must get her work done elsewhere. "You'll be sorry for that," said the enraged Tamson, "for in a short while I will see to it that you have no work to do." Then she left him, muttering. At that time four men were employed in the shoe maker's shop, including Paynter's informant who, some time later, went to America and remained away for about four years. On his return to the West of Cornwall, he visited his old employer and found him packing up his remaining goods prior to leaving the country. On being asked for an explanation, he said that his work had begun to fall off after Tamson had ill wished him, so it was no good staying any longer. He had lost practically everything that he once possessed.

Of course stories like the latter could be easily explained by natural means. It may be that Tamson had "put the word round" about the cobbler and so people were afraid to visit him and give him their trade. Even if this were so, it demonstrates the power and charisma of Tamsin among her contemporaries.

10

Even in her later years when she was confined to her bed, Tamsin's powers appeared not to diminish. A man living at Camborne related to Paynter how sometimes people were brought to her on stretchers and laid by her bedside entirely helpless. Then, after a short while, they would "rise up and go down the stairs perfectly well." Another account, recorded by MEJ in the Old Cornwall Journal, records how when Tammy was very ill, a farmer came to her for help. His horse was in great trouble and would die if not assisted. As Tammy was too ill to be moved, she called her little boy to her side (Tamsin had a son, probably by her marriage to Jemmy) and touched him, saying certain words. Then to the farmer she said "If you can carry my child to where the horse is, his touch shall cure it, for I have passed on my power to him for this occasion." He did as he was told and the horse recovered.

Perhaps the most detailed account of one of Tamsin's rituals is to be found in William Bottrell's collections of "drolls", published in his three volume collection of folk tales in the 1870's. Many of the tales retold by Bottrell, an inveterate collector of folk tales, were gained first hand from the lips of the old droll tellers whom he met in various pubs throughout the west of Cornwall. "The Ghost of Stythians" is one of hist most entertaining pieces and relates the story of the search for An Jenny Hendy's missing treasure. Bottrell subtitles the tale with these words: "This story is true in its main incidents, though the names, for obvious reasons, are fictitious." It is interesting that Bottrell has not fictionalised Tammy's name, nor that of her husband. Presumably he felt he was on safe ground since the Helston witch died on Oct 6th 1856 and her husband had died in 1874, a few years before the publication of Bottrell's volumes of tales.

In Bottrell's (semi-fictitious ?) tale, An Jenny dies and Robin, a relative, decides to call upon Tammy for assistance in trying to find An Jenny's missing will and treasure. The story is useful to us because Bottrell is a master of conveying character through dialogue and we gain an insight into the business like approach of the Helston wise woman when Bob or Robin asks her to clear up the mystery. Tammy replies:

"But you must know that it is a dreadful thing to undertake, and I shall want some money - two pounds at least - that we may get herbs, drugs, and other things not easily procured, for the sake of securing myself and you against any evil influences of the spirit, and that we may either put her to rest or send her to torment those who have stolen the money. If you can give me a pound now, to get what we want, I'll have all ready to rise the spirit some time next week, if you will."

It is clear that Tammy was an astute business woman. It is also evident that she must have been at the top of her league to have charged £2.00 - a large sum of money, bearing in mind that the average labourer's weekly wage in the late Victorian period was no more than ten shillings a week ! By today's standards Tammy would be charging something like £500 or more. By pellar standards this would mean that she had something like a 100% success rate - hence her widespread and enduring reputation.

There is also an indication in the story of the method Tammy used to conjure the spirits, for she mentions the purchase of certain drugs. These would be hallucinogenic compounds, presumably, to assist her communion with the spirit world. It is interesting that in India even today much the same method is employed by female soothsayers when they wish to commune with the spirit world or divine the future.

After a vain attempt to raise the spirit of the deceased and during which Robin almost dies of fright, it is decided that his cousin will take his place. Having arrived at Stythians churchyard (near Helston), Tammy then begins to summon the spirit. There follows a wonderful description of her: "The witch, stretching out her arms, her red cloak and grey hair streaming back on the wind, pointed with her staff towards the place whence these frightful sounds proceeded, and said: "Behold, it cometh: be thou prepared !" What then appears is a hideous figure in a shroud which turns out to be none other than Jemmy Thomas in full ghoul regalia. However, the ruse is seen for what it is, Jemmy is soundly beaten and the three extra sovereigns paid to Jemmy and Tammy are duly returned to them. Only slightly repentant, Tammy then suggests a practical method by which to obtain the missing money:

"Now listen to me. I have been thinking of a plan, and ef thy with, Jack, es equal to thy courage, this sperat-risan may be turned to some account for Bob, after all. The story es gone round far and near that Robin was going to employ me, and that An Jenny was to be called up; but few doubt my power to do et; so let's give out now that she has appeared, and declared to us who have taken the money, and farther, that unless the stolen money and other things that belonged to her, are brought to her late abode, within a month, her sperat will haunt them, and the white witch shall mark them so that all the world may know them by one blind eye; and anything more may be said, that can be thought of as likely to frighten the cousins into doing what we wish." The result of this ruse is that those who had owed An Jenny money were only too quick to repay Robin and settle their debts. The twist of the story occurs when we are told that some months afterwards when repair work is done on the thatch roof of An Jenny's cottage, the will and some jewellery are discovered.

Bottrell's story has all the hallmarks of a tale that is in its essence true and it is more than likely that Tammy and Jemmy worked together as a team in the early days of their marriage. The story is useful because it not only demonstrates how highly paid and regarded Tammy was in her own community but we also gain a glimpse of her powers in action. It appears that she was an all rounder and that her powers encompassed divination, necromancy, healing, distance healing, the removal of spells and herbal lore.

Although Tammy died in the mid century her reputation still lives on, although few of the younger generation in Helston remember her. Yet for there to be such a variety of folklore memories and reminiscences about her to have survived for over a hundred years after her death leads one to realise that in the middle of the last century the influence of the pellar, cunning man or wise woman held considerable sway over the common populace.

DOLLY PENTREATH

Dolly Pentreath is perhaps best remembered as one of the last living links with the Cornish language. Yet few remember or honour her name as a Cornish wise woman or witch. She was certainly influential within her own community and much feared and respected by the people of Mousehole and Newlyn.

Dolly or, to give her her real name, Dorothy Pentreath was born one Dorothy Jeffery in or around the year 1700. Despite a thorough search being made (by W.T. Hoblyn, OCS Vol 2, 7, pp 7 - 11) of the Baptisms and Burials contained in the Registers of the parish of Paul there was no trace found of her birth being registered in that year. Two entries were found, the first being "Dorothy, daughter of Nicholas Pentreath (and Joan), baptized at Paul Church, 16 May, 1692. " If this is the Dolly we are looking for, then that would make her 85 when she died in 1777. The other entry was for one Dorothy Crankan, who married Dick Pentreath. This woman was more commonly known under the name of "Nanny Nicholls" than by "Nanny Pentreath." This was the woman who married Nicholas Pentreath at Paul Church in 1706 or 1707. It seems likely that it is the former Dorothy whom we are interested in. In the last century it was quite common among some Cornish women to refer to themselves by their maiden and not their married name, so this may not surprise us.

In his article on "The Probable Parentage of Dorothy Pentreath", W. T. Hoblyn relates how he managed to track down in Mousehole (in 1934) a Mr John Halse who knew a family called the Blewetts. The Blewetts, who also lived in Mousehole (the elder Blewett was baptized at Paul church on the 22nd June 1744), knew Dolly well and in brief, his information was thus:

"Dolly Pentreath was never married; she lived at one time in a small court, now torn down and replaced by a good granite building, occupied (Aug., 1934) by a hairdresser and tobacconist named Ladner, overlooking the bank, at its middle point, of Mousehole harbour. Dolly removed to the house opposite the "Keigwin Arms" where she died in 1777."

This information tallies with the Paul baptismal register which states (under the year 1729, for October 18th): "John, base child of Dolly Pentreath was baptized." This would place Dolly in her late twenties when she had her illegitimate (base) son.

The Blewett account goes on to offer the following information about Dolly:

"She was dirty about her person and habits and very coarsely spoken when she chose. She had an illegitimate child, of which no further information could be given. As regards Dolly's age at decease, this was certainly not the reputed 102 years; it was probably less than 90 years."

This description tallies with the picture often given of women who, in the last century, were regarded as "witches". They were usually widows or single women and sometimes people who had transgressed the rules of society in some way. They would often be women who lived alone and who could even be of independent means. Above all,

An early woodcut study of Dolly Pentreath,
witch and fish seller. Probably drawn from life.

they were women who followed the traditions of the wise woman and that might include divination, midwifery and the casting or removal of spells. In Dolly's case the fact that she was bringing up an illegitimate child suggests that she might have been regarded as an outsider and one who had defied the regulations of the parish by rearing a "base" child on her own.

How did Dolly earn her living ? We know from the Borlase family that Dolly used to sell fish at Castle Horneck and she no doubt plied her trade in this manner, picking up her stock from the Newlyn fishermen. However, like a great deal of Cornish fish women at the time, this would not have been her sole source of income. Fortunately William Bottrell,the folklorist, has left us with a considerable amount of information regarding Dolly and her activities. According to Bottrell, Dolly belonged to "one of the most ancient and respectable families in the parish of Paul". He also claims that she lived in Duck Street and there was visited by a number of scholars of the day because of her knowledge of the Cornish language.

According to Bottrell and Daines Barrington, one of the scholars who interviewed Dolly at length and who communicated the account to John Lloyd, a member of the FSA, Dolly was most certainly a follower of the Old Religion and was skilled in fortune telling. According to Bottrell:

"Dolly, from her skill in fortune-telling, charming for the cure of various diseases, giving directions to the young folks as to the best way to try for sweethearts, and other practices of divination, came to be regarded as one of those who have acquired so much forbidden knowledge that they have the power to blast or ban, to lay a spell on man or beast, so that the old dame was little loved, but - what is the next best thing - much feared as one of those overwise ones about whom we now often hear the whisper, accompanied by the ominous shake of the head... "That she knows the hour and the minute: on that account it is much better not to offend the one who holds the dreaded secret. This mysterious intimation alludes to the general belief that there is an hour in every day, and a minute, only known to the demon-taught, in that particular hour (which varies from day to day) in which as we say "curses will not fall to the ground." This notion seems to be some vestige of the dogmas belonging to judical astrology, perhaps the shadow of some idea about the culmination of the malignant planet. However that may be, the belief exists to the present hour; also that our pellars, conjurors, white witches, or by whatever name these wise people are distinguished, have aprofound acquaintance with this mysterious science. It seems that Dolly was also regarded as one having this knowledge, and more fearful kinds of wisdom, by the stories still told of her. When much excited, she seemed to forget the little English she knew; and her voluble Cornish speech, then imperfectly understood by the younger and educated folks, impressed the people with far greater terrors than if she cursed or scolded in a language of which they knew the import."

Bottrell's view of Dolly emphasises the strength of her reputation as a wise woman and witch who, it seems, had the undoubted power to both heal and curse. Like many witches of the period, she was certainly feared for her knowledge of occult matters and to hear her curse in Cornish must have been a fearsome experience.

Bottrell tells a story about Dolly which reinforces the apprehension people experienced when meeting her.

"One day Mr Price, of Choone, was riding down Newlyn Hill on a shying, restive horse, when Dolly the Spring (as she was more generally called than by her right name) was slowly hobbling down the narrow lane (then a mere bridle path) before him. Dolly's broad beaver hat, scarlet cloak, and cowal, as she resolutely kept to the middle lane, left less space than Mr Price or his horse thought sufficient for them to pass beside her. The gentleman, wishing to get ahead of Dolly, called out to her, "Clear the way !" Dolly would neither move on any faster, nor start apeg, as she said, for all the cursed Jamaica drummer's brats in the country, and told the gentleman that, like all other upstart beggars, he would ride to the devil, with much more of the same kind in her choicest English (which she could speak pretty well when cool). This civil talk, for Dolly, was not much to Mr Price's taste, and as he did not wish to be treated to any more of the popular history about the rise of his family, by the vigorous use of whip and spurs, he forced his horse to pass Dolly, but, in going by, the horse or rider came in contact with her cowal, full of fish, which was overturned and all the contents cast out into the muddy ditch. Dolly then forgot her English, and began to abuse in her native Cornish, which came more glibly from her tongue; at the same time casting mud, fish, and stones at Mr Price as hard and fast as she could pelt them, the refrain of each sentence of abuse being an oath ending with, "Cronnack an hagar dhu."

"As Dolly was reputed to be a kind of half witch, , as mentioned before, Mr Price became terribly frightened at hearing what he dreaded might be some horrible incantation for laying a spell on him and his, he endeavoured to appease her by paying for the fish, when she became a little more placable. He wished above all to know what she had been saying, to curse or blast him perhaps ? Dolly called him a fool for thinking of anything of the kind, and assure him that she was no more a witch than himself. Still, Mr Price was not satisfied, and before he arrived at the bottom of the hill, returned again to Dolly. He must know the meaning of what she repeated like a spell, after every oath, which he did not mind, as he could swear as hard and fast as she could in honest and plain English. At last he offered Dolly half-a-crown to be told the meaning of "Cronnack an hagar dhu." "Give me the money first then," says Dolly, "and I must call ye a fool for your pains; as all I said was to call ye a fool for your pains; as all I said was to call ye the ugly black toad that ye art."

"Mr Price, on hearing this, threatened to horsewhip her. Dolly then dared him to lift but a finger against her, and if he did, she would put such a spell on him as should make his arm rot from his shoulder, and began again to jabber Cornish, which so frightened Mr Price, or his horse, that they went off with all haste and left Dolly to gather up her fish in peace." '

Bottrell concludes that this anecdote was told to him by an old lady of Sennen who added that the Pentreath family were "remarkable for possessing more than the ordinary quantity of mental endowments."

The story is a wonderful example of the energy and power of the Crone. Note that she claims not to be a witch for in those days it was thought not only politically incorrect to be a witch but also dangerous. Hence the use of the name "pellar" or "wise woman" - but never "witch". However, once challenged, she reveals her ability to curse and cause real harm to the person who has caused her much offence. Note also that she wears a scarlet cloak. The scarlet cloak was always a sign at this period that the wearer was a witch of condiserable power.

Perhaps the most detailed account of an interview with Dolly was recorded in 1773 by the Honourable Daines Barrington, a gentleman scholar who travelled into Cornwall to ascertain whether the Cornish language was still spoken. In a letter written to John Lloyd he records this account:

"I set out from Penzance, with the landlord of the principal inn for my guide, towards Sennen, or the most western point; and when I approached the village I said that there must probably be some remains of the language in those parts if anywhere, as the village was in the road to no place whatever, and the only alehouse announced itself to the last in England.

"My guide, however, told me that I should be disappointed, but that if I would ride about ten miles about on my return to Penzance he would conduct me to a village called Mousehole, on the western side of Mount's Bay, where there was an old woman, called Dolly Pentreath, who could speak Cornish fluently. While we were travelling together towards Mousehole I inquired how he knew that this woman spoke Cornish; when he informed me that he frequently went from Penzance to Mousehole to buy fish, which were sold by her; and that when he did not offer her a price that was satisfactory, she grumbled to some other old women in an unknown tongue, which he concluded, therefore, to be Cornish.

"When we reached Mousehole I desired to be introduced as a person who laid a wager that there was not one who could converse in Cornish; upon which Dolly Pentreath spoke in an angry tone for two or three minutes, and in a language which sounded very like Welsh. The hut in which she lived was ain a very narrow lane, oposite to two rather better houses, at the doors of which two other women stood, who were advanced in years, and who I observed were laughing at what Dolly said to me.

"Upon this I asked them whether she had not been abusing me; to which they answered, "Very heartily" and because I had supposed she could not speak Cornish.

"I then said that they must be able to talk the language; to which they answered that they could not speak it readily, but that they understood it, being only ten or twelve years younger than Dolly Pentreath.

"I continued nine or ten days in Cornwall after this, but found that my friends whom I had left to the eastward continued as incredulous almost as they were before about these last remains of the Cornish language, because, among other reasons, Dr Borlase had supposed in his Natural History of The County, that it had entirely ceased to be spoken. It was also urged that, as he lived within four or five miles of the old woman

17

at Mousehole, he consequently must have heard of so singular a thing as her continuing to use the vernacular tongue.

"I had scarcely said or thought anything more about this matter till last summer (1772), having mentioned it to some Cornish people, I found that they could not credit that any person had existed within these few years who could speak their native language; and therefore, though I imagined there was but a small chance of Dolly Pentreath continuing to live, yet I wrote to the President, then in Devonshire, to desire that he would make some inquiry with regard to her; and he was so obliging as to procure me information from a gentleman whose house was within three miles of Mousehole, a considerable part of whose letter I subjoin.

""Dolly Pentreath is short of stature, and bends very much with old age, being in her eighty-seventh year, so lusty, however, as to walk hither to Castle Horneck, about three miles, in bad weather, in the morning and back again. She is somewhat deaf, but her intellect seemingly not impaired; has a memory so good, that she remembers perfectly well, that about four or five years ago at Mousehole, where she lives, she was sent for by a gentleman, who, being a stranger, had a curiosity to hear the Cornish language, which she was famed for retaining and speaking fluently, and that the innkeeper where the gentleman came from attended him.

("This gentleman," says Daines Barrington, "was myself; however, I did not presume to send for her, but waited upon her.")

""She does indeed, talk Cornish as readily as others do English, being bred up from a child to know no other language; nor could she (if we may believe her) talk a word of English before she was past twenty years of age, as, her father being a fisherman, she was sent with fish to Penzance at twelve years old, and sold them in the Cornish language, which the inhabitants in general, even the gentry, did then well understand. She is positive, however, that there is neither in Mousehole, nor in any other part of the county, any other person who knows anything of it, or, at least, can converse in it. She is poor, and maintained partly by the parish, and partly by fortune-telling and gabbling Cornish."

Four years after this account was written Dolly was dead. She was buried in the churchyard of the parish of Paul and an epitaph was written for her in both Cornish and English:

Coll Doll Pentreath cans ha Deau;
Marow ha kledyz ed Paul pleas -
Na ed an Egloz, gan pobel bras,
Bes ed Egloz-hay coth Dolly es.

Old Doll Pentreath, one hundred aged and two,
Deceased, and buried in Paul parish too -
Not in the Church, with people great and high,
But in the churchyard doth old Dolly lie !

The epitaph was never inscribed on her tombstone and the stone which was subsequently erected which stands against the churchyard wall was set up by Prince Louis Lucien Bonaparte in 1860. It reads: "here lieth interred Dorothy Pentreath, who died in 1778." In fact she died on December 26th 1777 and was buried the following day. The tombstone still exists and may be seen in the side of the churchyard wall, facing the road.

There is one other story about Dolly which gives substance to her reputation as a fearsome and powerful incarnation of the Crone. It is told in J H. Harris's book, Cornish Saints And Sinners. One one occasion a deserter from a man of war fled to her house for refuge. Dolly, seeing that there was a cavity in the chimney of her house large enough to conceal him, thrust him into it, lit her fire and filled the kettle with water to boil. In the middle of the kitchen she drew a "keeve" which she used for washing and when the naval officer and his men burst into the tiny cottage they saw her sitting bare legged on a stool, her skirts drawn up to her thighs and her feet ready to be plunged into the keeve. She screamed abuse at them on entering and said she was waiting for the water to become hot enough so she could bather her feet. The officer persisted in searching and Dolly abused him and cursed him in Cornish. She then rushed to the door and screamed to her neighbours that the officer and his men had invaded her home and were likely to ransack every other house in the village of Mousehole. The officer and his men immediately withdrew and left empty handed. That night a fishing lugger was seen stealing out of Mousehole harbour with the deserter on board. This tale is one of my favourite as it demonstrates not only the fierce Crone energy of Dolly but her tremendous courage in defending the underdog of Cornish society.

The memorial to Dolly Pentreath. Paul churchyard, near Penzance. Photo: The Author.

BETTY TRENOWETH

In the last two hundred years the small village of St Buryan in the far west of Cornwall has been a place renowned for witchcraft. Quite close to the village itself, on the way to Sennen and Land's End lies the little hamlet of Crows An Wra which is Cornish for The Witch's Cross. St Buryan itself is a place of remarkable atmosphere where it seems that time has literally stood still over the centuries. The Church has been established here for centuries and in medieval times the village was the centre of an order of priests who were fiercely independent - so much so that they were threatened with excommunication. This was also the setting of the remarkable film Straw Dogs - made in the 1960's, featuring Dustin Hoffman. This strange and brutal story chose as its theme the idea of the outsider who is not made welcome by the local community who "keep themselves to themselves".

In the last century St Buryan was home to one of the most famous and influential of Cornish witches, Dame Betty Trenoweth. Like many witches of her period, she spent much of her early life in service to "gentle folk" but in later years she plied her trade in the West of Cornwall and built up a fearsome reputation as a healer, wise woman and fortune teller. Although "official" records about her life are scant, stories about her were common among the "droll tellers" of mid-nineteenth century Cornwall and there is no reason to doubt that she existed since nearly all of Bottell's characters can be traced to real families in the west of Cornwall just prior to the time he was collecting his tales. Fortunately, during the 1860's William Bottrell, an ex-school master from Penzance, was responsible for collecting most of the stories relating to Betty and preserved them in Volume Three of his "Traditions And Hearthside Stories of West Cornwall". This remarkable collection of tales about local characters in the Penwith area contains amusing stories about local people at a time when Penwith was still isolated from the rest of Cornwall and when the position of the wise woman in Cornish society was much esteemed.

It appears that much earlier in her life Betty Trenoweth worked at Trove Mill (near Lamorna - the modern and very misleading spelling is Trewoofe) where she was responsible for grinding the corn brought to her by the people of St Buryan and the outlying hamlets. At that time Trove was owned by one Squire Lovell who earned a reputation as a ne'er do well. The subject of the Lovells' lives and reputation was made into an old Christmas play which was performed in the early part of the last century. The play also featured the characters of Father Christmas, and the Devil. The main thrust of the play concerns Duffy, a young woman, who marries Squire Lovell, but who is secretly in love with a young man called Huey Lenine. Duffy befriends Betty, the "kind old witch" and confides in her that she is deeply unhappy with her marriage to the Squire. The old crone advises her to be patient and to feather her nest so that she will, in time, secure the hand of Lenine after the Squire has died. Meanwhile Duffy enlists the help of the "Buccaboo" (otherwise the Devil !) to spin wool, blankets and home-made cloth. Betty then decides to provide her friend with further assistance:

"Duffy my dear, cheer up ! I wouldn't like for 'e to be taken away before me. Now do what I advise 'e, and it is much to me if we don't find 'e a way to fool this young devil yet, he is but a green one. So, tomorrow evening, soon after sunset, bring me down a black jack of your oldest and strongest beer. But before that, be sure you get the Squire to go hare-hunting. Fool with him the old story, or anything else to make him go. Wait up till he comes back, and note well what he may say. Go 'e home now; ask no more questions !"

After persuading her husband to go hunting a hare after dark, Betty stops the water mill, puts on her steeple-crowned hat and red cloak and makes her way to the fogou between Trove and Boleigh. (The fogou is today just a ruin and lies on the road which wends its way past the Merry Maidens stone circle.) After midnight the squire returns in an excited manner to the manor house and there begins to relate to his young wife this most extraordinary story:

"We hunted all the way down... from Trove to Lamorna without seeing a hare. We turned to come home and, up by Bosava, out popped a hare... She (the hare) took up the moors; we followed close through after, through bogs, furze and brambles, helter-skelter, amongst mire and water. For miles we chased her - the finest hare that ever was seen, most in the dogs' mouths all the way, yet they couldn't catch her at all. By the starlight we had her in sight all the way up the Bottom, between Trove and Boleigh; there we lost all sight and scent of her at last, but not till, tearing through brakes of brambles and thorns, we found ourselves in the Grambler Grove. And now," continued he, after a pull from the flagon , "I know for certain that what old folks say is true - how witches meet the Devil there of summer's nights. In winter they assemble in the Fuggo Hole, we all know; because one may then often hear the devil piping for their dance under our parlour floor - that's right over the iner end of the Fuggo. And now I believe that what we took for a hare was a witch that we chased into this haunted wood. Looking through the thickets I spied, on a bare spot, surrounded by old withered oaks, a glimmering flame rising through clouds of smoke. The dogs skulked back and stood around me like things cared. Getting nearer now and looking through an opening, I saw scores of women - some old and ugly, others young and passable enow as far as looks go. Most of them were busy gathering withered ferns or dry sticks to the fire. I noted, too, that other witches, if one might judge by their dress, were constantly arriving - flying in over the trees, some mounted on ragworts, brooms, ladles, furze-pikes, or anything they could get astride of. Others came on through the smoke as comfortable as you please, sittingon three-legged stolls; and alighted by the fire, with their black cats on their laps. Many came through the thickets like hares, made a spring through the flame, and came out as decent lasses as one might see in Buryan Church of a holiday. A good large bonfire soon blazed up; then, by its light, I saw, a little way back, sitting under a tree, who should 'e think ? Why, no less than old witch Bet, of the mill. And by her side a strapping dark-faced fellow, that wasn't bad looking andthat one wouldn't take to be a devil at all but for the company he was with, and the sight of his forked tail that just peeped out from under his coat-skirts. Every now and the Old Bet held to his mouth a black leather jack, much like ours, and the Devil seemed tolike the liquor by the way he smacked his lips... The Devil got drunk at last by the way he capered when the witches, locked hand in hand, danced round the fire with him in their midst... The witches, locked hand-in - hand, danced madder and faster, pulled each other right through the fire, and they weren't so much as singed, the bitches. I wanted to dance

22

with them and called out as I advanced, "Hurra ! my merry Devil, and witches all !" In an instant, as quick as lightning, the music stopped, out went the fire, and a blast of wind swept away the embers and ashes, a cloud of dust and fire came in my eyes and nearly blinded me. When I again looked up they had all vanished. By good luck I found my way out of the wood and home. I'll have another hunt tomorrow and hope for better luck."

The story goes on to relate how the Devil then visits Duffy and demands that she return to his kingdom with her. However, when Duffy speaks his secret name, "Tarraway", he disappears in a puff of smoke and blaze of lightning. Of course, Betty is accused of witchcraft by the Squire and Duffy is shut up in a small room and forced to spin wool as a penance for her mischief.

This old Cornish droll has many interesting features. Betty is called by different names in the story. She is known variously as "Betty", "An Joan (Aunt Joan)". Sometimes she is also called Chymellan - presumably a corruption of "the place of the mill." She reveals that thirty years previously she had been married and was then living at Trevider. At that time she was a weaver, as were many women of her station. She also did agricultural work to help earn a living, which included "branding turves, raking tabs (roots, grass, etc), making an arish mow (bale of straw). Her mistress was then a woman called Madam Pendar "a noted spinster." She also reveals that she sustained an injury through excessive spinning and we may imagine her to have been lame.

Betty again crops up in another of William Bottrell's drolls entitled "The Story of Nelly Wearne." In this long and complex story we learn how the illegitimate daughter of "the last Cardew of Boskenna" met a sailor at the St Buryan fair on a night of storm and rain. After the storm Nelly, Captain Black and his companion have disappeared. Local people put down the diappearance to demonic intervention but they are proved wrong when, years later, an "elderly foreign-looking woman, whose dres was of rich stuff and of outlandish make", appears in the village and asks after Betty Trenoweth. At this point in the narrative Betty is described as living on the Trevorgans side of the town of St Buryan. When Betty (who is described as a relative of Nelly's) recovers from the shock of seeing Nelly, the latter then unravels a long, complicated story of her adventures with Captain Black which includes pirates and shipwrecks and much besides.

There then follows a wonderful piece of Crone machination for Betty then decides to take advantage of Nelly's changed and aged appearance in order to drum up a bit of business. She says to Nelly: "Tis as good as a play, my dear, to see how all the old women of Church-town try to discover who and what you are, and they can't find out, because, for the fun of the thing, I take good care to fool them.... I told them that you were a Wise Woman come from the East - that you ramble over cliffs and moors to gather herbs, whilst morning dew is on them, or when the moon is near to full - that no one can beat you in making from them, ointments, salves, and still-waters - that you understand all sorts of complaints and can cure anything, from the gripes to the palsy. And now all the young wenches in the parish want to know if you can read fortunes; they think you can because yuo look like a gipsey, so they say. "Why yes to be sure; nobody better, " I told them. Now listen to me," Betty went on to say, when she had recovered her breath, "I've made them believe that you can read the stars - that you know all that will happen to any body by the lines of their palms - that you can tell, by means of rushes, spring water and ivy leaves, and scores of ways besides, who are to be married, as well as who are to die unblessed with a husband. And to everything they asked about your knowledge of white witchcraft, I assured them that you knew more about magic, conjuration and so forth, than the Witch of Endor that we have all heard of."

Naturally Nelly , unskilled as she is in the ways of divination, asks how she can keep up the pretence of being a fortune teller. No problem, replies Betty, "You know everthing remarkable that ever happened in the families round up to the last twenty years or so, and what you don't know I can tell 'e. When they find that you're acquainted with what's past they are sure to believe that you can read them the future."

Nelly soon masters the art of fortune telling under the careful scrutiny of Betty and the two enjoy a widening reputation as wise women. Eventually Captain Black makes a miraculous appearance and, as they say, everyone lives happily after.

Interestingly, Bottrell goes on to record that about the time of Captain Black's reunion with nelly, Betty "became notorious as a witch and her practice of the black art was discovered and put past doubt by some one in Church town against whom she had a grudge." A certain villager who had blamed his failing cattle on Betty's ill-wishing, determined to punish her. So he made her image in clay or dough and then ran a long skewer through the lower part of its body. His friends who were privy to the plot went to visit Betty and saw her fall to the ground, where she writhed in agony, crying out: "What's in my body ? I can hold out no longer ! Run over to Dick Angwin's and tell am I'll make et up weth am ef he will !" Fearing Betty might die and leave her curse on them unbroken, they made friends with Betty and then destroyed the image.

Bottrell then tells the story of how Betty once went to Penzance market where she saw a pig she wished to fatten through the winter. However, she offered less for the pig than Tom Trenoweth, a cousin of her's, who bought it. Very miffed, Betty then threatened him with these words: "Ef I don't have thee shust wish thy cake dough, and find the sow the dearest bargain thee hast ever had." Tom refused to give up the pig and Betty went off mumbling.

Over the months that ensued it became clear to Tom that the sow was steadily getting thinner. So Tom then decided to take it back to Penzance to sell it at the market. When he got to Bojew Bottom the pig escaped and then dragged him through the mud and over the moor. Eventually he got a rope round its neck but as he was making it secure a hare jumped out from behind a bush by Tregonebris bridge and the pig bolted, taking Tom with it. Once in the stream under the bridge the pig would not move so Tom sat by the road, disconsolate. Eventually Betty appeared and looking as if butter wouldn't melt in her mouth, asked Tom what he was doing there. He explained and then said to accuse Betty of witchcraft with these words:

"The sow is under the "brudge" and thee dust know it well enow. For who but thee crossed the road and went over the moor in the shape of a hare ?" Betty then suggests that she might give cousin Tom half the value of the sow since the animal is now but skin and bone and Tom reluctantly agrees. Betty walks off and the sow follows her like a dog.

Another wonderful tale Bottrell recorded about Betty was "The Story of Madam Noy" in which Betty scores a decided victory with the close fisted "termagant", Madam Noy. This story of social rivalry and point scoring begins with an encounter between Madam Noy and Betty. Betty asks Madam Noy if she might have a dozen eggs from her stock of poultry. Madam Noy, tru to form, replies she won't even think of it since,if she has refused to sell them to her own sister, "dust thee think that I would sell them to the likes of you ?" "I don't care a cuss whether you do or no", Betty replies, "but if you won't sell me some eggs you shall wish your cake dough." Madam Noy, becoming heated, calls her a deceitful old bitch and throws a stone at her. Enraged, Betty ill wishes her with these words:

Mary Noy, thou ugly, old and spiteful plague,
I give thee the collick, the palsy and ague.
All the eggs thy fowl lay, from this shall be addle,
All thy hens have the pip and die with the straddle.
And before nine moons have come and gone,
If all they coppies (chickens) there shan't live one;
Thy arm and thy hand, that cast the stone
Shall wither and waste to skin and bone.

From that day onwards the chickens failed Madam Noy and the curse succeeded. Bottrell goes onb to say this:

"'Tis said that Betty owed her proficiency in the black art to her frequent conferences with Old Nick (or her familiar, whatever his name might have been) who almost nightly took the form of An Mally Perase's black bull, and under that shape met the witch on the northern side of Burian churchyard.

Bottrell's account of Betty Trenoweth conveys the myths of his age: the notion that there were black as opposed to white witches (witches never described themselves thus. These terms were used by the educated of the age, and Bottrell had received a classical education and taught as a schoolmaster in Cornwall and abroad); the idea that a witch was in league with the Devil, itself a nonsense invented by medieval Christian theologians to justify the existence of suffering and evil in the world. However, if we consider the stories themselves, they are convincing in the way they show the witch's ability to curse when spurned or used badly by other members of her community and the way that Betty, like all solitary hedge witches of her age, sought the company of a younger woman and trained her as a worthy successor in the Craft.

25

JOAN WYTTE

Until recently, in the famous Witchcraft Museum in Boscastle, North Cornwall, lay the remains of a woman who is still, to some extent, steeped in mystery. The extraordinary story of Joan Wytte, or The Fairy Woman of Bodmin Town, was revealed to me by the present curators and owners of the museum. Graham King and Liz Crow who purchased the museum from the renowned occultist and collector Cecil Williamson.

On close examination, the bones appear to be those of a small woman and they have been very crudely linked together. Until recently, when the museum was under Mr Williamson's charge, the skeleton hung unceremoniously in a museum case in front of a coffin but it was then laid on its side and moved to a location upstairs where it subsequently reclined on an ornate cloth.

Mr Williamson told me that the skeleton was obtained from an antique dealer within the area of North Cornwall many years ago. The story of her life is yet incomplete but is in itself remarkable for the light it throws on the way women were treated in an age of comparitive barbarity and few medicines.

Joan Wytte was born in Bodmin in the year 1775 but lived for only thirty eight years. Like may witches she died in prison. In her day she was known as the fighting fairy woman of Bodmin town. Fairy, perhaps, because she was a tiny person in stature but perhaps also because of her ability to commune with the spirit world - an ability she may also have shared with Anne Jefferies from St Teath, another witch featured in this book.

Joan (a common witch's name !) was probably brought up, like the rest of her family, as a weaver and a yarn twister. Certainly her ancestors had pursued this craft since 1524 when town records record a John Wytte as a weaver. However, in the late eighteenth century the demand for weaving and yarn twisting had declined and the Wyttes had gone into "tawning" or making white leather, a trade which enjoyed some prosperity in Bodmin since white leather was much in demand by the eighteenth century gentry

Although Joan pursued her career in this fashion she was also renowned in Bodmin for her clairvoyant abilities and could accurately predict the future of the clients who came and visited her in the back street where she and her family lived. Close by to the Wytte house was a holy well called Scarlett's well where young Joan would often visit to make offerings to the Goddess and scry the waters with her younger clients who sought guidance in the affairs of the heart. In the Midsummer she, like others of her craft, visited the well and tied clooties or "jawns" on the branches of the old hawthorn tree that grew there. As the strips of material which had been torn from the diseased limbs of her clients decayed, so, it was imagined, the limbs would heal because of the healing powers of the Goddess of the waters. Much later, in the nineteenth century, Dr Thomas Quiller-Couch, father of Sir Arthur Quiller-Couch, the famous writer,had the waters of the well analysed and found that it was rich in natural flourides.

In her youth Joan was of a temperate and kind disposition but once she had passed the age of twenty something happened to her which was to change her life tragically. She developed tooth decay which penetrated into her right wisdom teeth. In our own age she would have received treatment for such a painful condition but in the early 1800's there were few dentists to be found. At first she learned to eat on the other side of her mouth but the pain grew worse and eventually an abscess formed, poisoning the whole jaw. Joan's behaviour began to change. Gone was the happy young woman her parents had known. She continued her craft of spells and divination but now she began to be feared. She began to shout at her clients for no reason which could be apparent to them. Sometimes she would pick a fight with people she scarcely knew. On occasions she could be heard shouting and moaning during the night so that people believed she might be possessed by the Devil himself. Her freedom of the town ended one lamentable day when she got involved in a fight which ended with her lifting and beating people three or four times her weight and size. So grievous were their injuries that she was arrested and brought before the town magistrates of Bodmin.

By now the reputation of Joan was fearsome. She was feared and hated by many who had no knowledge of the pain she had endured. And al the time the poison in her jaw worried away at her, driving her to drink and delirium

At the assizes she was found guilty of grievous bodily harm and found to be of unsound mind. She was committed to Bodmin Gaol. Conditions in Bodmin Gaol at that time were appalling. Prisoners who were without wealth had no special privileges and were treated as less than human. Within a short space of time the cold, dank communal area where Joan was kept with dozens of others started to break down her body. Already weakened by pain, she was made, like the others, to work on the treadmill until she reached the point of utter exhaustion. Her meals were little more than a thin gruel diluted to the consistency of water. Because of her fearsome reputation, many of the other prisoners left her alone and this was at least something of a blessing.

Finally, at the age of thirty eight Joan succumbed to the bronchial pneumonia which was the bane of so many prisoners' lives. With few if any prison visitors around at this time in the history of the prison service, the medical needs of prisoners like Joan were rarely a consideration of the prison governor and his staff. When Joan died she was a thin as a rake. Her diet had been little more than stone ground flour for years on end. For years she had smoked a short clay pipe, one of her few comforts. Her hands were slender and her fingers were claw like. She had fought like a tiger with the warders so that finally they had learned to leave her be. In an interview with the Bodmin newspapers the governor, one James Chappel had said "Yes, I admit that we have had women that we could not tame, but never a man." He was referring, of course, to poor Joan.

By an odd quirk of fate, in the very same year that Joan was born, 1775, elsewhere in Bodmin town one William Clift was born nearby to Berrycombe Hill. The Clifts were millers, William's father having died when he was very young. Hard times ensued but

JOAN WYTTE
BORN 1775
DIED 1813
IN BODMIN GAOL

BURIED 1998

NO
LONGER
ABUSED

Memorial stone to the memory
of Joan Wytte, the fighting "fairy"
woman of Bodmin. Photo: The author.
Courtesy, Graham King, Museum of
Witchcraft.

William's mother managed to get her studious son a place in the poor house school. Here William proved to be a most able pupil, demonstrating many skills. He was good at mathematics, but his real forte was drawing. Mrs Clift was acquainted with a wealthy family known as the Gilberts. When William finally left school she asked Mrs Gilbert if her husband might give her son a place in his establishment. Mr Gilbert obliged and it was not long before Mr Gilbert realised that young William had a remarkable talent for drawing. Now the GIlberts had a very close friend called John Hunter, a man famous for his collection of medical specimens now known as part of the Hunterian Museum at the Royal College of Surgeons in London. Young William Clift was promptly sent to London and there was apprenticed to John Hunter and given the job of making drawings of thousands of medical speciemns and strange anatomical deformities. Eventually Hunter died and Clift took over the museum and became the official curator.

Many years passed. Clift married and had children but eventually he worked so intensively that he placed himself under a great strain and suffered a nervous breakdown. He travelled down to Cornwall with his wife to stay with his friends the Gilberts at their house in Bodmin. This was in the year 1813, the very year that Joan had died in Bodmin gaol. William subsequently met John Hamley, the surgeon in charge of the gaol. One afternoon John showed Clift his strange collection of plaster casts of heads taken from the inmates of the gaol and the death masks which had been made of the men and women who had been executed there. William Clift was fascinated by these heads. One of the heads was that of poor Joan whose body was lying in the prison mortuary. Clift heard about Joan's amazing strength and fierce independence and when he had viewed the corpse he asked if he could have it removed to the Hunterian Museum where it could be dissected. However, poor Joan's body never made it and was dissected, instead by Hamley. So the skeleton, when it was finished, was consigned to the prison store rooms and forgotten about. Until, that is, the new prison governor came to Bodmin.

The new governor was one William Hicks, a raconteur, practical joker and eccentric. So well known was Hicks that after he died a series of reminiscences and stories of his were published. There is a photograph of him showing him to be a tall, rotund man with a twinkle in his eye. Hicks was a bombast of the first order but he was entertaining.

One evening Hicks prepared for a dinner party. After dinner had been taken and the port and cigars had been consumed, Hicks asked his guests to adjourn to an adjacent room. As the guests took their seats, they saw that in the dimly lit room they were facing what looked like a coffin. Hicks then explained that they were going to take part in a seance in which the skeleton of Joan would provide the medium. All the questions would be answered by a tap from the good lady's coffin. One bone was placed in Joan's coffin (this for the raps), one was held by the person who would recieve the "yesses" and the other by the "no" person. Offstage, meanwhile, Hicks had an accomplice to play Joan's part by providing her raps. The seance had barely got under way when the door to Joan's coffin opened, there was an almighty whoosh and the three bones were wrenchesd out of the people's hands and they then flew about the room with terrible violence, hitting the heads and shoulders of the participants.

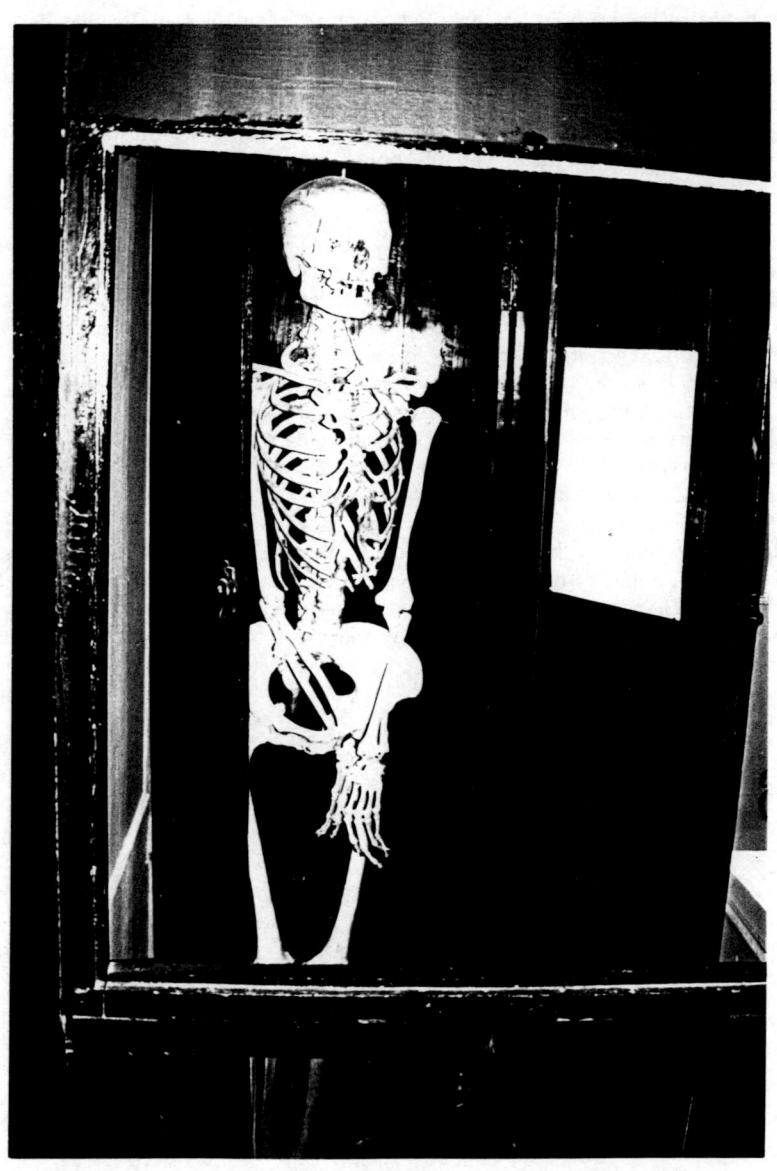

The skeleton of Joan Wytte, the Fairy Woman
of Bodmin. For many years her remains lay
in the Museum of Witchcraft at Boscastle.
Photo: The author, courtesy, Graham King.

Joan's bones were returned to the medical store room at the prison where they remained until 1922 when the naval portion of the prison was shut. In 1927 the entire prison was closed by an order in council and the skeleton of poor Joan was passed to a doctor who had a practice in North Cornwall. It was via the doctor that the skeleton, and its remarkable story, came into the hands of the museum. A forensic examination was later conducted on the bones and it was concluded that Joan had been in long contact not only with natural flouride but also with china clay.

The present curators of the Witchcraft Museum experienced a variety of poltergeist phenomena regarding Joan's bones. Perturbed by this and by the tragic story of her life and death, they attempted to discover exactly what Joan's wishes might be, for clearly it was not fitting that her remains should be on public view for much longer. It became clear that the spirit of Joan would not rest until she was given a proper burial. In September 1998 the Independent Newspaper reported that Graham King, the proprietor of the Museum of Witchcraft, had decided to take Joan's bones out of the display case and bury her "somewhere in the woods" at an undisclosed location. He had, it was reported, "a magical spot" in mind and was seeking the local landlord's permission. The funeral rite would be "very simple and respectful" and he was going to take out the metal that was tying her bones together in order to place the bones in a wicker basket lined with wool. Included in the grave were simple grave goods, including s mall bottle of brandy, a clay pipe, a bit of tobacco and some magic herbs "to help her on her way." The ceremony was conducted some time later and a special marker stone was commissioned from a German sculptor which may still be seen in the museum today. Thus ends the tragic story of Joan Wytte.   .

ANNE JEFFERIES

Thomas Tonkin wrote in his volume "Natural History" (published in 1727):

"Many strange stories we have, more especially among the miners, of Fairies or, as they call them, Piskys, Small People &c., of their discovering Mines to them, playing on Musick very sweetly in them, &c, Dancing in Rings and Circles, from whence come the many bare rings and circles which we see in many places, particularly in a field of my own on Trevaunance, called the Rose Field, where I have been told of above 20 several appearances of them even in the day time. But as I look upon them alll as perfect whimsies and dreams, I shall say no more of them".

Tonkin, like many rationalist thinkers of his age, was writing about seventy years after the case of Anne Jefferies, the famous Fairy Woman of St Teath. He, like many of his contemporaries, had begun to discount and dismiss what he regarded as invention and superstition. Only what was visible was real and fairies were the invention of women. He goes on to discuss a case from his own experience:

"I remember that about 40 years since, viz. about 1687, one Agnes Martin of St Agnes, pretended that she had been carried away by these Small People, and gave a long account of her living among them, &c., and that her employment was to look after the children. I have often discours'd her about it since that time, she being now dead, and by the best conjectures that I could make she was carried away by a gang of gipsies (for she was certainly wanting several years, and no one could tell what was become of her, till she was accidentally met with in a Fair and brought home), and being very young, not above 7 or eight years of age, carried about from place to place generally by night, &c.,; she verily believed the tale she told, and that she lived with them underground, was very well treated by them, and (no doubt) had this story put into her head by them. I mention this little story as being within my own knowledge, and not unknown, neither, to many people still living, who have had it from her own mouth..."

Did Agnes really live with the fairies ? If she did not, then how do we account for the large number of tales similar to this collected by William Bottrell from the lips of the old Cornish droll tellers ?

Since Tonkin does not see fit to give us the details of young Agnes' life with the fairies we shall never know it to be true or false. However, about 40 years earlier and even more remarkable story, that of Anne Jefferies, provided much more detail and in this case the evidence is certainly most convincing for the link between witches, clairvoyance and psychic healing.

Anne Jefferies was born in St Teath, North Cornwall, a tiny village not that far from Camelford, in December 1626. The tiny cottage in which Anne was brought up is still in existence. Since she was a poor man's child (her father was an agricultural labourer), she was sent to live with the Martyn family. It was here, as she grew to be a teenager, that she first realised that she could not only see but commune with the fairies

Most of our information about Anne comes from an account of her life contained in a document published by Moses Pitt, a London publisher. Pitt asked his nephew, a lawyer, to interview Anne about her life since she had been unjustly imprisoned by the notorious magistrate Tregeagle, about whom so many legends exist concerning his pact with the Devil. In September 1691 he wrote a letter to Pitt telling him that his sister's husband, one Humphry Martin, had interviewed Anne who was reluctant to talk to him about her experiences.

In Martyn's letter to Pitt, he reveals that Anne is still living at the age of 70 and is married to one William Warren, formerly a hind to the eminent physician, Dr Richard Lewes. In Martyn's account he tells of how Anne had been in the notorious Bodmin gaol for three months and lived for six months without eating meat. During that time she had performed several cures (presumably on other inmates). Two years later Pitt wrote again to Martyn and asked him to interview her once more. Martyn wrote back to Pitt on the 31st January 1693 saying that he had seen Anne. He had spoken to her at length but she was reluctant to tell of her story for fear that the publisher would "make books or ballads of it." Such was her fear of the justices at the assizes that she imagined she might again be arrested and imprisoned for what she had said. She also remarks that all the people she once knew in St Teath are dead except for one Thomas Christopher, a blind man.

Martyn then relates all that he knows of the case from his friends and relatives

Having been passed into the protection of the Martyn family, Anne grew into a lively and courageous teenager. When she was nineteen years old, she had been sitting knitting in an arbour in trhe family's garden when she was suddenly aware of a collection of six tiny people, all clothed in green coming over the hedge towards her. When the family heard what she had said, they brought her into the house and put her to bed, but as soon as she recovered, she sat up and cried out: "They are just gone out of the window ! Do you not see them ?"

Martyn gives the impression that during this period Anne is suffering from some kind of traumatic condition for he refers to it as a distemper. During the weeks that followed Martyn's grandmother died but the family kept this news from Anne, for they feared it might unhinge her. (this was in the April of 1646) During this period Anne became very ill and "could not stand on her feet" and she became "even as a changeling". As soon as she began to show signs of recovery, or gain strength, she would spread her legs as wide as she could she would support herself on the edges of chairs and tables, but if anything vexed her she would "fall into fits and continue them for a long time, so that we were afraid that she would have died in one of them."

Eventually Anne recovered strength enough to pay a visit with the family to St Teath church to pay her devotions to God. Soon after this, however, occurred the first example of her ability to administer psychic healing.

One afternoon in the harvest period, we find Anne and Martyn's mother alone in the house together, the men being out in the fields harvesting Martyn's mother is anxious to obtain flour from the local mill so that she can ask her maids to bake fresh bread. She could not leave the house for she had the feeling that Anne might set fire to the house, for she was still very weak at that time. At last Martyn's mother persuaded Anne to walk with her in the gardens The mother then leaves, announcing her intention to walk to the mill, locking Anne out of the house.

On her way to the mill, the mother falls and twists her leg. A neighbour, riding by on horseback, hears her cry out and lifts her onto his horse, returning her home. Then, as soon as she laid to rest, the reapers are alerted to what has happened and they return from the fields. A man servant is then despatched to fetch a Mr Lobb (a surgeon from Bodmin) However, before he departs, Anne enters and tells the mother she is very sorry for the accident, describing to her in detail where it hapened and in what manner. She then demanded to see the injured leg,:

"Upon which Anne took my mother's leg upon her lap and stroked it with her hand, and then asked my mother if she did not find ease by her stroking of it ? My mother confessed to her she did. Upon this she desired my mother to forbear sending for the surgeon, for she would, by the blessing of God, cure her leg. And to satisfy my mother of the truth of it, she again appealed to my mother whether she did not find further ease upon her continued stroking of the part affected."

As Anne continues to heal the leg, she denies that she has been told by anyone where the accident had taken place, and she then confides in her guardian how she came to see fairies:

"You know that this my sickness and fits came very suddenly upon me, which brought me very low and weak, and have made me very simple. Now the cause of my sickness was this: I was one day knitting of stockings in the arbour of the garden, and there came over the garden hedge of a sudden six small people". This, says Anne, has caused her sickness. They continue their appearance to her, always appearing in even numbers - 2, 4, 6 or 8. When Anne was out in the garden, she tells the mother, the fairies visited her and asked if she had been put out of the house against her will. Upon Anne replying yes to this they declared that her guardian should not fare well from it and at that very instant the mother fell on the pathway and hurt her leg.

The cure of the leg and the stories about Anne and the fairies soon spread like wildfire. From all over the county of Cornwall people of all all ages, with all manner of sicknesses, sores, etc., came, even from as far away as Land's End. Anne took no money or reward from them. Neither did she buy any medicines or salves to cure the sick. Martyn recalls how from that day onwards for a year she forsake eating with the family, only breaking the habit on Christmas Day when she ate roast beef with them. Anne would also tell the family which people were coming to see her days before they arrived and at what time they would be arriving.

On one occasion Martyn had decided to speak with Anne. He went to her bed chamber but finding the door locked asked her to open the door. She replied: "have alittle patience and I will let you in immediately." When Martyn looked through the keyhole he saw her eating. And when she had done eating she stood still by the bedside and appeared to give thanks.

Another strange occurrence is cited by Martyn. One Sunday a neighbour visited the family home and asked for Anne. The family told him she was in her bedroom. The neighbour went upstairs but could not find her. As soon as he had told the family this fact, Anne came out of the bedchamber and told the neighbour that she was at that time in her bedchamber eating a meal and that she saw him enter and heard his voice but remained invisible to him.

Anne was certainly clairvoyant and would tell people what would befall them in a few days' time. On one occasion Martyn's sister was given a silver cup, which held about a quart but when she brought it to her mother she would not accept since the young girl had said it was a gift from the fairy folk.

Eventually Anne's reputation grew to such an extent that the neighbouring magistrates and ministers paid a visit to the house and they then questioned Anne in detail. By this time Anne had made a full recovery from her illness. The priest tried to persuade her that she had been consorting with the Devil. When the minister and the magistrates had left the house, Anne spoke to Martyn's father, saying "Now they call !", referring to the fairy folk. She repeated this comment twice more. She then went and fetched a Bible and said that she had been to visit the fairies. They had spoken to her, saying this:

"What, hath there been some magistrates and ministers to you, and dissuaded you from coming any more to us, saying we are evil spirits, and that it is all delusions of the devil ? Pray desire them to read in the 1st Epistle of St. John, chapter 4, verse 1, "Dearly beloved, believe not every spirit, but try the spirits whether they be of God." This is of great interest since Anne was quite illiterate !

The story goes on to relate how, after this incident, John Tregeagle, a Justice of the Peace, issued a warrant for Anne's arrest and sent her to Bodmin gaol where she was kept "for a long time" (we do not know how long. Unfortunately the gaol books for this period are missing.) On the day the constable came to arrest Anne, she foresaw the event whilst she was milking the cows and she asked the fairies if she should hide herlself but they replied in the negative. At the sessions which Anne attended,the constable, Giles Bawden was asked to give evidence as to her character. Martyn himself was brought before them and interrogated. he was asked if he secretly brought food to Anne in her bedchamber.

Anne then languished in Bodmin gaol "for a considerable time after" Tregeagle also had her removed and kept in his own house for a period of time during which he deliberately starved her to see if her claim about being fed by the fairies was actually genuine. At last, when she was finally discharged, Anne was not allowed to live with Mr Martyn. Instead she went to live with Mr Martyn (senior)'s sister, Mrs France Tom, a widow who lived in Padstow who took her in. During this latter part of her life Anne continued to cure people. In time she went to live with her brother and eventually married.

Trevorder, the home of Justice Tregagle, the man who placed Anne Jefferies under house arrest in order to discredit her reputation as a "fairy woman".

The story of Anne and the fairy folk has an interesting rider. Some time in the 1930's the author and scholar Hamilton Jenkin came across some manuscripts in the Bodleian Library at Oxford. They were dated February and April 1647. One of the letters contained these words:

"I can acquaint you with ... news... of a young girle which foretells things to come and most have fallen out true. She eats nothing but sweetmeats, as Alemans (almonds) comfited and the like, which are brought her by small people cladd in greene and sometimes by birds. She cures most diseases, the Falling sickness (epilepsy) especially and broken bones, only with the touch of her hands... She hath been examined by three able Divines, and gives a good accompt of her religion and hath the Scriptures very perfectly, though quite unlearned. They are fearful to meddle with her for she tells them to their faces that none of them are able to hurt her... At present she is at Bodmin, at the Mayor's house ... She says that the King shall enjoy his own and be revenged of his enemies.

The clue to Anne's long confinement can surely be read in this last sentence for if her utterances and predictions were at all political she might have been seen as a trouble maker who, in the popular mind, might be able to foretell the future of the monarchy.

Anne's treatment by Tregeagle was certainly barbaric and typical of the way in which wise women of the age were suspected of "being in league with the Devil." At the time of her career as a clairvoyant a number of treatises had been issued warning Justices of the Peace of the excesses of harsh sentences for witchcraft and no doubt Tregeagle had this in mind. It also entirely possible that he removed her from Bodmin and had her live at his house (a highly illegal practice even then) because he had amorous designs upon her. For that reason perhaps her final obscurity was a blessing and it would help to explain her reluctance to give interviews to publishers' agents. .

GRANNY BOSWELL

Anne Boswell was born in 1813. Her maiden name may have been Bottrell. She was probably of mixed Irish and Romany gipsey stock and as such inherited from her mother those arts of fortune telling and wise woman ways which had been in her family for centuries. She was born in Ireland and probably brought by her mother to England during the 1840's at the time of the great potato famine. According to one source she was employed as a lady's maid and was subsequently disowned by her family for marrying beneath herself. When Anne married her second husband, Ephraim, she married into a large and influential Romany family. There had been Boswells living in the area of Helston for many years. They set up their wagons in the area beneath the town now occupied by the boating lake and were, by all accounts, much disliked by the gentry of the town.

It was probably in Ireland that Anne learned at her mother's knee some of the beliefs and superstition that she was to pass on to her own children. It was also from her mother that she inherited the powers that she was to draw upon in later life - powers that were to sustain her in her craft. Superstition played a vital part in the lives of the Romanies. They believed that evil spirits roamed the night searching for victims and among the charms they carried for protection against these spirits were the holed stones, the breastbones of jays and kingfishers. To counteract the power of the "Evil Eye", talismans of bead-like fossils called adderstones were worn around the neck. To dream of blood or snakes, to hear dogs howling, to meet a squint-eyed woman or a donkey or a funeral on the open road - all of these things were thought to be bad omens. On the other hand, however, the moon brought good luck, small green frogs, pieces of coral, falling stars and white horses were all thought to be beneficial. Anne also learned from her mother that the Earth (De Develeski) is the Divine Mother of all existence. She is the supreme gipsey deity. For this reason, Anne learned to love and cherish the earth.

Like many women of her station, Anne worked on the farms which ringed the Helston area when she was young, and in the days when the agricultural cycle was truly seasonal, there was always something she could turn her hand to. Her day began early and finished late. An old woman recalled in the 1930's, writing about this period: "My father was a skilled labourer earning 9 shillings a week, with a good cottage and a garden, when I was a child in about 1850. We were allowed to keep two pigs for our own use, and also to gather as much faggot wood as we wanted from the hedges. Time was obtained to cut this by doing piecework, which began at 4 or 5 a.m.; the normal hours being from 6 a.m. to 7 p.m." In the fields Anne followed the routine of the other women from her community; weeding corn, picking stones, planting potatoes, rolling barley and oats, hay-making or reaping with the sickle. For such work she would receive no more than 6d or 8d. per day.

When she was older, possibly ine her thirties, Anne married Ephraim Boswell (also a Romany). He was seven years older than Anne and the son of "Old Boswell,", otherwise known throughout this part of Cornwall as "The King of The Gipsies". Like all gipsies, their marriage ceremony embraced the tradition of jumping over the broom together and clasping each others hands while an elder of their community sprinkled salt over them. After this they went through the civil ceremony. They had six children, Unity (1861 - 1892), born when Anne was 48 years old, Agnes-Mary (1863 - 1951), Lillie, Maria Abraham and Henry, born when Anne was in her late forties. The births were difficult for Anne and her plight became no less bearable. In many cases such children rarely survived their tender years but Anne had the gift of her inheritance and was skilled in the ways of administering cures. On one occasion the Boswells were offered temporary accommodation in a cottage but they did not last there. A description recorded in 1836 gives us a picture of how life was for the children of the poor in such circumstances. "I found little Kitty and her cripple brother (the latter no better than a baby) packed into the window seat brandishing a knife from one hand to the other, and then scuffling for its possession," wrote Mrs Pascoe, after visiting a farm labourer's cottage in the year 1836. "The young, seven year old housekeeper, meanwhile, was lighting the fire with a piece of tallow, making repeated excursions to and from the fireplace and the cradle in order to "borrow" a handful of straw from the baby's loose palliasse, and leaving a trail of combustibles each time."

If Anne suffered from the burden of her children, her husband suffered equally. Like many others of his station, he could rarely afford proper clothing to protect him from the harsh winter weather. He wore a coarse shirt, a pair of "duck" trousers which did not quite reach his ankles, a waistcoat, a smock and low quartered shoes, without socks or stockings.

In winter, when the fields were sodden with water and mud, Ephraim would tie a "thumb bind" to his legs, straw rope which was wound round from the top of the knee to provide him with some form of insulation. When he came home in the evening soaked to the skin, he would dry himself by the fire. But in the morning he would put on the same clothes again which were often still icy from the cold. By the age of fifty he had become rheumatic (small wonder) and was obliged, like many men of his class, to walk on sticks.

Despite all these hardships, Anne or Granny Boswell, as she came to be known, was much revered for the wisdom which she might impart among the members of her community. She was the first to whom young girls would make their way in the matter of gaining sweethearts. She was acquainted with innumerable charms, many of which had been transmitted to her by her own mother. Many of those who were sick from the scrofula were given a small linen bag which contained several spiders. She instructed her clients to hang this bag in their bed chambers. As the spiders died, so they would recover. Many of her clients were young women who sought happiness in finding a partner. These she would instruct as follows: On the evening of the first Friday of the month you must go take off your shoes when going to bed, place them in the form of a letter T, then walk upstairs backwards without a word being spoken. You must then take off your apron, fold it in three folds and put it under your pillow, saying these words:

"On Friday night I go to bed,
A threefold apron under my head.
In my bed I wish to sleep,

Granny Boswell. Taken in the 1880's by a Helston photographer.
Courtesy Helston Folk Museum.

In my sleep I wish to dream,
In my dream I wish to see,
Who my true-love is to be.
Let him be by sea, let him be by land,
Let him come by my bedside and stand.
Let him be dressed in apparel or dressed in array,
Let him come in the clothes he wears every day."

On other occasions people would visit Granny Boswell because their calves were suffering from ringworm or some other disease. She would ask for half a crown and then encircle each ringworm three times against the sun. By the next evening the infected places would be dry again. On other occasions people would visit her in great distress, fearing that they had been ill-wished by someone. Granny Boswell would ask them to try and obtain a photograph of the ill-wisher and, if this could be procured, the victim would be asked to write that person's name across the photograph and the whole thing would be thrown into the fire, thus breaking the spell.

Despite Anne's reputation and achievements as a wise woman, tragedy was to befall her children, to whom whe often behaved harshly (One of her descendants reports being beaten with a stick whilst being abjured in an accent comprising a misxture of Irish and Cornish). Her youngest son, Henry, died at the age of twenty one - young even for those hard days, whilst her daughter, Unity Bailey, died at the age of thiry one. However, the greatest tragedy in her life concerned her older son, Abraham who died a convicted murderer.

Granny Boswell was to outlive not only her sons and daughter but also her husband, who died at the respectable age of 84. After his death Granny Boswell seemed to grow even more outrageous than she had appeared to be when she was younger. Like many crones of that time, she was both respected but also feared, for she had the power not only to heal but also to curse. One story will suffice to prove the point.

Some years ago the author of this work came across a fascinating document - an unpublished memoir of Captain Taylor. Taylor's father was a doctor who worked in the Helston area in the early part of this century and father and son lived at No 1 Cross Street. It was election time in 1906. At that time Granny Boswell was ancient indeed - 93 years of age. In that year the Taylor's were working hard to put the Tories back in office and they were busy ferrying people back and forth to the polling station in Coinagehall Street in their newly polished motor car. Let Captain Taylor take up the story:

"In the 1906 election ... we were ferrying voters to the poll; I remember that the polished brass paraffin headlights were adorned with large blue bows. My father had reversed the car across the street outside our house, and was about to go forward in the other direction, when the local witch walked in front. She stood there, a ragged and grimy old hag, apparently fascinated by the shining and throbbing machine; and swaying slightly, as on election day she was more drunk than usual. My father, to make her move, first shouted, then roared the engine and tooted the horn. This nettled her, and she shrieked in her broad Cornish and with much foul language that

41

the qualified wagon wasn't going to get as far as the other end of the qualified street; she turned her back, and stalked off in fury. We started; before the car was half-way down the street there was a loud snap, and one of the one-inch steel tension-rods broke clean in two. A horse towed us home. It had long been said that Granny Boswell could ill-wish cattle and fowls, and she lived largely on the gifts of those who desired to ensure that her eye should be averted from theirs; but to be able to ill-wish a motor car in public was a most startling confirmation of her art, and on the strength of that, I have no doubt, she was able to live in comparative luxury for the rest of her life."

This remarkable story (amusing as it is) demonstrates that even among the middle classes of Helston the power of the 19th Century witch was regarded as absolute. Sadly, however, the doctor's predictions about Granny living in comparative luxury was merely an idle fancy. Her husband deceased, Granny Boswell had entered into a period of comparative poverty. In 1902, when she was 89 years old she attempted to enter the Helston workhouse. However, when her case was heard before the borough bench in February 1902, it was decided that she had no claim on any place for a settlement and consequently the guardians of the Helston workhouse refused to accept her as an inmate. In an article in the Cornishman for the 27th February of that year the journalist comments that "the only way she could be well cared for and prevented from giving so much annoyance would be for the townsfolk to petition for her."

So this lonely and remarkable figure lived out the remainder of her days, almost reaching the century before she died in 1906. She lived largely on the generosity of other women who wished to avoid abortions or being ill-wished by her and she was widely known for her excessive drinking in the pubs of Helston, especially on Feast days, when she would get drunker than usual. She would often be seen in Meneage Street, sitting on a ledge outside a shop window, puffing at her clay pipe in deep contemplation, no doubt considering the vagaries of her own fortune.

One incident clouded her life above all others. In 1883 a brutal murder was committed on the highway not far from the village of Cubert. Two men, one Thomas Down, aged about 40 - an itinerant razor-grinder and Abraham Boswell, aged 20, a chair-mender and Granny Boswell's son, arrived at Hosken's public house at about noon on a day in October. They drank a considerable amount of brandy and during the afternoon Boswell, a rough and powerful looking fellow, started a quarrel. After this he spent the rest of the afternoon alone at a table, sitting in silence and staring into the middle disrance with a hammer in front of him. The dispute which was to lead to murder had begun some days previously in the famous Blue Anchor in Helston where the beer was (and still) powerfully strong and where the company was often of a dubious nature.

Both men left the pub at 4pm and made their way in the direction of Newlyn East, Down with his grinding machine on his back and Boswell carrying a bundle of canes. Shortly afterwards Down was kicked to the ground by Boswell who battered him to death with his hammer. Boswell belonged to a band of gipsies who had travelled widely in Cornwall for many years. When the case came to trial Boswell was found guilty of murder and presumably condemned to death. Was he hung the following year and his body buried in unconsecrated ground ? I had thought this to be the case but it apears that his sentence may have been commuted. The facts here remain a mystery. According to information recently received by one of Granny Boswell's direct descendants, he subsequently married one Selina Smith and had 4 children. There is also in existence a photograph of Abraham standing at the door of his tent with two of his sons, taken in c. 1919.

When Granny Boswell died, her funeral was a grand affair. In the gipsey tradtion death, like birth, must always take place outside the caravan. So Anne was taken outdoors shortly before she died. After her death, fellow gipsies took her most treasured possessions, her gold coins and lucky amulets, and placed them inside her coffin to ensure that she would have a comfortable existence beyond the grave. Granny Boswell was buried in the little churchyard at Tregerest, near St Just, where her grave may still be seen today.

The tradition of the Romany gypsey in Cornwall followed by Granny Boswell did not die with her. Two subsequent practitioners, Mary Hearne and Harriet Richards, both fell foul of the law as a result of practising their ancient craft.

At the Cornwall Assizes, on October 27th, 1927, Mary Hearne, aged 68, and described as a "hawker of no fixed abode", was found guilty to a charge of demanding by menaces from Richard Harris Paddy, a gardener from St Mawes, sums of money amounting to £179 10s.. The claim was that she had obtained the money by "pretending to exercise a certain kind of witchcraft sorcery or enchantment."

According to the report published in the Falmouth Packet of that year, Hearne obtained the money by stating to Paddy that an illness from which he was suffering had been caused by his being "overlooked", this being an effect of the "evil eye." Paddy was a man of some 60 years who had spent nearly all his life at St Mawes. He had known Hearne for at least 25 years and they had enjoyed a close relationship during that time, Hearne commenting in her evidence that "he was just like a husband to me for twelve years."

According to Hearne's statement, he had given her small sums of money in order to support her, the largest of these sums amounting to no more than £40. Paddy's evidence, which was read out in court on his behalf, stated that "the woman played about with a compass, which she passed over Paddy's hand, talked about the planets and Venus, and was creating the right atmosphere. No black cat appeared on the scene or anything of that kind as was once done by these charlatans." According to Paddy's evidence, she had threatened him that if he refused to pay the money, he would go blind and become a bed lier. Eventually, however, his health became so bad that his employer questioned him and the whole business then came to light. Hearne was found guilty and subsequently sentenced to six months imprisonment.

One would have liked to known more about this case, which bears a strong similarity to many of the 17th century accounts brought before magistrates in Cornwall and Devon. Although the evidence against Hearne appeared to be circumstantial, it was accepted without question by the magistrate. As with so many cases of this kind, there was a long-standing relationship between the accuser and the accused which turned sour. It was then that witchcraft was used as a means of exacting revenge upon the woman.

One of the most fascinating witchcraft cases in more recent times, however, concerns a 72 year old gipsey woman who lived at Hendra, just outside St Kew, in North Cornwall. Harriet was accused of defrauding and deceiving a farmer and his wife who lived at Penhale. The case was a curious one. Richards appeared at two special sittings of the Wadebridge magistrates to answer 15 charges.

It was claimed by the farmer, Mr Osborne, that Richards had obtained the grand sum of £297 from him under false pretences over a period of two to three years. As the case was reported in the newspapers, it became obvious that this was no ordinary case of straightforward fraud. The ancient Richards was the seventh child of a seventh child and therefore possessed the power to "work the planets" and to vanquish evil spirits which had been attacking the farmer. Osborne and his wife had been experiencing a great deal of misfortune. There had been serious losses on the farm and his wife had given birth to a still-born baby.

During the trial it was revealed that Richards had turned up at the farm one day when Mrs Osborne was alone. She determined that the Osbornes had experienced much grief and offered to help them for a small sum of money. This was then agreed upon. Mrs Osborne noted that the old woman seemed to radiate a strong energy and appeared to be transfixed by her gaze. From then on Harriet's visits became more regular. She sold the Osbornes a special rug which she then asked them to pace and make wishes to send away the evil spirits that had been dogging them. She also agreed to "put money on the planets" in order to increase their fortunes.

Over the next year Harriet's visits continued. So noticeable did they become that local neighbours declined to visit the farmer and his wife, for they feared the reputation of the Romany witch. During the ensuing period Mr Osborne gave Richards turkeys and other fowl and he also lent her sums of money which he claimed added up to £600. All of this Richards subsequently denied in court.

The whole basis of the prosecution case was that Mrs Richards was taking advantage of Mrs Osborne's ill-health and the considerable anxiety of Mr Osborne over his wife's condition. She had, it was claimed in court, convinced the couple that their ill fortunes were caused by ill wishing. Mrs Osborne had been unwell at the time that Richards first called on them and had really believed that the old woman had the power to change her fortune. During the trial Mrs Osborne stated: "I believed all the stories she told me, that I should have lost the baby, my husband would have lost me, and that he would have been in an asylum. I thought that if we bought the rug with the three wishes, everything would be alright."

Eventually Richards did admit, under police interrogation, to obtaining small sums of money under false pretences, although it was agreed that no one could be precise about the total sum of money that was involved. In her defence, Richards claimed: "I have the power to remove evil spells and spirits by putting money on the planets." The method that was used was an interesting one. Richards would arrive at the house bearing small pieces of paper which she would then burn on the fire, whence small explosions would ensue.

On June 28th 1954 the baby was born and Mrs Osborne returned home in July. On August 21st Mrs Richards paid the Osbornes a visit and is reputed to have said: "If it had not been for me you would not have had the baby alive. I have been working on the planets day and night and you can see what I have done." The child later fell ill. Richards called again and told them: "I could see it in my crystal, and I have worked day and night on the planets till she was better." The Osbornes then paid her £38 for her services.

Richards tried to make reparation and paid back the couple £150. She was placed on probation for three years and ordered to pay a further £100 within 28days by way of compensation. Richards' health had suffered as a result of the proceedings against her. Her husband had had a serious operation from which he had not fully recovered and the accused was to have an operation for a cyst on her head. She claimed to have pleaded guilty because she could not endure a long trial. Richards counsel claimed on her behalf that both she and her husband were quite illiterate and that they had been married for about 50 years. She had had 14 children, about 100 grandchildren and a number of great grandchildren. The whole of her life had been spent in a tent.

The judge concluded that she was an old woman but that she had committed a "very cruel fraud" on the Osbornes." ..You created a sense of fear in the people upon whom you prayed," he went on.

In the end Richards left the court a free woman and her fourteen sons and daughters split the costs between them.

The case provides us with an interesting late example of the percieved power of the witch in modern society. It appears that Harriet was a witch in the oldest sense of the term. She was an old woman with undoubted powers who was paid to remove a curse and who expected to be paid for her undoubted abilities. She seemed to possess some charismatic power. Like women accused of witchcraft in the 17th century, she shared an intense relationship with the accuser and there was a longstanding exchange of goods prior to the accusation being made. Did she really exercise power over the Osbornes ? I believe that she did, for why else would she have gone on for so long unchallenged by the husband ? There is no doubt in my mind that the Osbornes had an implicit belief in her powers and that they were prepared to support her craft in order to alleviate their suffering. I suspect that things turned sour when they realised that their fortune had not greatly improved in the way they had hoped for. What is intrinsically fascinating in this late case is the light it shows on the special bond between the witch and her client and the percieved power possessed by the witch. The vulnerability of the witch, her position as an outsider within the community - these are all factors which make one feel one is not dealing with a case from the twentieth century at all.

THE TONKEN AFFAIR

One of the most extraordinary witchcraft cases which has survived in pamphlet form is that of the Tonken Affair. At the Morrab Private Library in Penzance there is a copy of this pamphlet which apparently was acquired by W. Borlase, the famous Cornish antiquarian and amateur archaeologist. It was printed in London by George Croom in 1686 and is bound up with a print of Matthew Hopkins, the self styled "witchfinder general." According to the document one John Tonken (a common name in Penzance and the surrounding area), a youth of 15 or 16 years, was the subject of a dramatic bewitchment by two women.

The account states that Tonken was the subject of sudden fits and that on 4th of May, 1686, as he lay in bed, a woman in a blue jerkin and red petticoat appeared to him, telling him that he would not get better before he had vomited up a selection of nutshells, pins and nails. The youth shared the information about this apparition with several people but none saw what he evidently had done. He subsequently vomited up three pins, half a walnut shell and in the next few days, threee more shells, and some more pins, some of which were crooked.

The woman appeared to him on a number of subsequent occasions and the boy would shriek out that the woman was putting things into his mouth and threatening to choke him. He called out the name of Jesus and refused the apparition. Sometimes he would lie as if dead and at other times he would show signs of levitation. He continued to vomit up a variety of items including an ear of rye and great quantities of straw and rushes, some of them a yard long with broad knots on them. Nails and more pins, numbering 16 or 17 in all were then vomited up. At other times he said the woman had pricked him in the heel and when the bedclothes were pulled back his attendants found a threepenny mail attached to his heel. He also brought up dry bramble, and several pieces of flat sticks.

Several people must now have heard the sensational news for the report goes on to say that some visitors tried to search his mouth to see if it was all a trick, though they found nothing. The woman then told him that she would kill him if she could, whereupon the boy asked God to prevent this. In one of the fits someone noticed that the youth was staring fixedly at the thatch. The person thrust his sword into the thatch but the boy cried out that the apparition had escaped into a corner like a mouse

At one point in the proceedings he brought up a huge needle called a beeting needle which was half an inch broad and an inch and a half long, much to the amazement of his uncle, one Edward Plimrose. The boy subsequently cried out to his audience that he wanted to be well again and implored them to help him, though significantly he neither knew the name of the witch who had done this to him nor her address. He even offered the person who could identify the witch five pounds. At this point he was able to number not one but three women in his ramblings, "whereupon he cried out "What a confederacy !" Upon this being said the witch troubled him no more. Two days after this the boy made a rapid recovery and was able to get about the streets of Penzance on a pair of crutches. An affidavit was at some time later sent

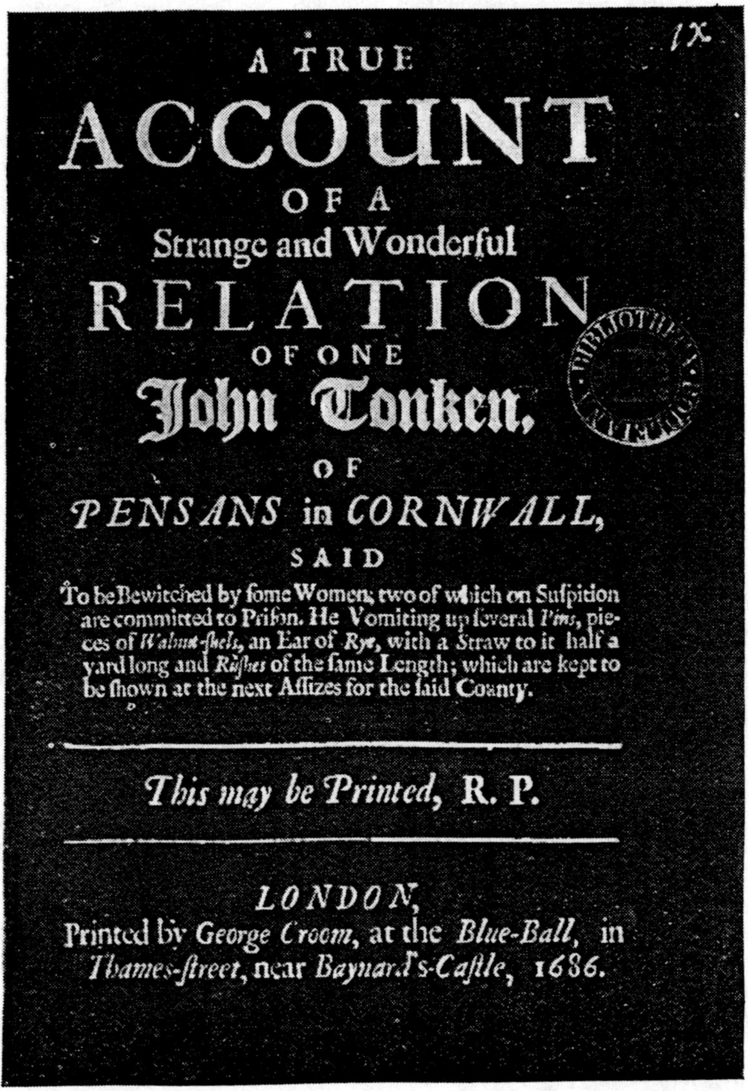

A TRUE

ACCOUNT

OF A

Strange and Wonderful

RELATION

OF ONE

John Tonken,

OF

PENSANS in *CORNWALL*,

SAID

To be Bewitched by some Women; two of which on Suspition
are committed to Prison. He Vomiting up several *Pins*, pieces of *Walnut-shels*, an Ear of *Rye*, with a Straw to it half a
yard long and *Rushes* of the same Length; which are kept to
be shown at the next Assizes for the said County.

This may be Printed, R. P.

LONDON,
Printed by *George Croom*, at the *Blue-Ball*, in
Thames-street, near *Baynard's-Castle*, 1686.

The rare pamphlet regarding the bewitchment
of John Tonken of Penzance, published in 1686.
This sensational case led to the imprisonment of
two women at Launceston Gaol.

48

before a justice by several people and three women were arrested and sent to Launceston Gaol, charged with maleficia, namely Jane Noal (alias Nickless), and Betty or Elizabeth Sneeze. The document ends with the hope that these "old women" may be found guilty at the next assizes.

This was in fact not the only case of "hysterical possession" or delirium inspired by witchcraft from the Cornish record. In 1696 one Mary, wife of Johann Guy, was sent to Launceston, accused of bewitching Philadelphia Row. It was deposed that Row, who also vomited pins, straws and feathers, often saw the appearance of Mary Guy (An Historical Essay, F. Hutchison, 1718, p.44)

What are we to make of the Tonkin case ? In fact cases like this were not uncommon at the time and in the witchcraft annals there are several examples of child possession and hysterical behaviour associated with the fear of a witch.

Twenty years earlier, for example, Rose Cullender of Lowestoft, a widow and Amy Dunn, the same, were charged by Sam Pacy for bewitching his daughters. The two women were arrested, orally examined and searched for marks or teats. When the Pacy daughters came to Bury for the indictment to be heard they "fell into strange and violent fits, screeking out in a most sad manner" and were unable to speak again until the women were convicted. When Rose Cullender was refused some herrings by his wife, his daughter Anne became "sore afflicted in her stomach" and vomited up pins. In her swooning she frequently saw the apparition of Rose Cullender Diana Bocking also testified that her daughter Jane had pains in the stomach and daily vomited crooked pins.

Pins were also mysteriously conveyed into the palms of her hands. More sensations followed. Mary Chandler's daughter, 18 years old, was so frightened by the sight of Rose Cullender in court that she was struck blind and cried out "Burn her ! Burn her !" When Margaret Arnold had the Pacy children to stay with her, she discovered that they raised between them no less than 30 pins. They also used to see mice running round the house.

The children declared that the pins were brought into the house by means of bees and flies. On one occasion a child threw into the fire an invisible mouse and "there did appear upon it, like the flashing of gunpowder, though the Deponent saw nothing in the child's hand". More circumstantial evidence appeared from other townsfolk, most of it petty and questionable. Summing up, Sir Matthew Hale proclaimed that the women were indeed witches for witches certainly existed, as the scriptures confirmed. Moreover, to let the guilty go free would be an "abomination to the Lord". Judgement was pronounced and the two prisoners were hanged, despite the fact that they "confessed nothing."

The Lowestoft case was fairly typical of many witchcraft cases of the time. There is the usual catalogue of hysterical behaviour and the putting on of a performance by the accuser. Much of the evidence is provided by the parents and then the net is cast wider to include neighbours. Exactly what inspired young Tonkin to behave in this way we shall never now know. Perhaps it was some private grievance or a dispute with the two women. In the Lowestoft case it appears to be the case that one of the accused was in the habit of applying for alms at the household of the accusing family. Whether or not Jane and Betty were released we also do not know, though it is fairly likely that they were, since there is no evidence of an assize record or pamphlet literature apart from the one already cited."

Cases of possession achieved a degree of notoriety in the middle ages among closed communties like that at Loudun in France. There was often a degree of theatricality to them, as was true of the Penzance incident.

THE MUSEUM OF WITCHCRAFT

In these days of post-Gardnerian Wicca, it is comforting to know that there is one place in Britain which seeks to uphold the history and traditions of witchcraft. It is even more fortunate that such a place should lie in Cornwall. The Museum of Witchcraft lies along the harbour road towards the sea in the little village of Boscastle. For some years now it has been in the capable hands of Graham King, a former businessman who purchased the premises and a proportion of the artefacts from its previous owner, Cecil Williamson. Since Cecil Williamson's retirement, the Museum has undergone numerous changes, including the removal and burial of the bones of Joan Wytte, already referred to in this book. Apart from holding an unrivalled collection of artefacts relating to the work of numerous west country witches, collected over a lifetime by Cecil Williamson, the premises' upstairs section has an impressive library and archive section which is available by consultation for serious researchers of the subject of witchcraft.

The museum is the only one of its kind in the UK and is a remarkable testament to the craft of the witch. It is particularly strong on artefacts collected during the 19th and 20th centuries. The innovations have included representative displays relating to the work of modern followers of wicca and information relating to some of the 19th Century practitioners described in this book.

Many of the visitors who perambulate through the museum's corridors daily in the spring and summer months may be unaware of the history of the place or of its illustrious former owner. Cecil Wiliamson is perhaps the most enigmatic and remarkable of all modern witches. Unlike Gerald Gardner, whom he knew intimately and assisted, he shuns publicity and is adamant that the approach taken by Gardner and his successors is largely a diversion from the true craft of the solitary witch. An avid opponent of many of the forms of modern paganism, he is justifiably proud of his collection, which spans a lifetime of experience and knowledge.

Cecil was born in 1909 into a well to do family. During the First World War his father, who was a naval officer, was given a number of postings. Consequently Cecil was sent to a number of prep schools and during the summer months, he was sent to various relatives for holidays. One summer he stayed with an uncle, the Reverend William Fox, the Vicar of North Bovey, on Dartmoor where he met his first village witch and gained an understanding of the ancient craft. He also learned much of the occult from his grandmother, who was a well attested astrologer. He later attended Malden College and there was introduced to a well known Tarot reader and palmist, Madame de la Maize. After graduating from Malden College, Cecil then went to work on a tobacco farm in Rhodesia where he also met a retired witch doctor and learned much about the secrets of African Magic. He returned to London in 1930 and then worked on the production side of the film industry. It was during this time that he met many of the occult figures of the time, including Aleister Crowley and Margaret Murray, the renowned author of many books on witchcraft and lifelong folklorist. During the Second World War, Cecil was employed by the home office and was asked to set up a Witchcraft Resource Centre so as to monitor and combat the work of Nazi occultists. However, during the course of this work, it appears that

Cecil's interest in witchcraft deepened and he was given a wide variety of artefacts.

After the conclusion of the War, Cecil was at a loss as to how he might combine business with pleasure, so he decided to open a Museum of Witchcraft, selecting Stratford Upon Avon as a sound tourist centre. Once established, however, he received a great deal of opposition from local Christians, so he moved to the Isle of Man where he purchased a property at Castletown. It was here that Gerald Gardner, Britain's most famous witch, first came to stay with Cecil and, by all accounts, began a rather unhappy association with Cecil. This culminated in Cecil selling the property to Gardner and relocating to Windsor, where he was again unhappy enough to run the gauntlet of the Monarchy (or rather, its representatives !) He then relocated to Bourton On The Water where he was once again subjected to pressure from Christians to quit. Cecil promptly left and returned to the West Country, the scene of his earlier adventures. He set up a museum of Smuggling at Polperro and a House of Spells at Looe. It was in 1960 that he finally relocated to Boscastle and here he remained until 1996, gathering a vast collection of artefacts, many of which still remain in his possession.

Cecil's approach to the subject of witchcraft has been consistent over the 90 odd years of his involvement with the subject. He thinks little of Gerald Gardner and his reinvention of witchcraft and has done his utmost to collect genuine artefacts and memories of the true practitioners of the craft. The present museum truly reflects this preoccupation. To quote from his own pamphlet, "West Country Witches": "... the wayside witch today keeps a low profile, content to let her brave sisters in the cult and covens of Wicca... receive the full blast of hostile publicity. The Christians - thanks to the Jew Leviticus, still beat loudly on their drums of Anti-witchcraft hate and the media of press and television let loose their dogs to rush in and to grab the occult and satanic bones of sex-sin-and sensation as and when thrown to them."

The legacy of Cecil's research and collection is included in this study since the author believes it to be one of the few genuine contributions to the subject of West Country witchcraft which have been made in this century. The present museum provides an indispensible insight into the genuine witchcraft traditions of the last century and much is owed to the resolution and tenacity of its founder, Cecil Williamson.

An A-Z Of Cornish Witchcraft

The practice of witchcraft in Cornwall was once widespread if by "witchcraft" one interprets this is a set of beliefs and practices rooted in tradition and to which many people subscribed. In the past a great deal of emphasis has been laid on "witchcraft" as a historical or cultural phenomenon which existed prior to the Witchcraft Repeal Act of the 18th Century, yet not much interest has been given to the continued attention it deserved in the public eye from that time until the present. As anyone who studies the newspapers of that period will know, there is a rich harvest to be gained from such study. Several factors emerge. Firstly, it was not always the case that those described as witches were old but it seems to have been a common belief that witchcraft was somehow inherited through a family. Secondly, there was considerable interest in the idea of being cursed and the means by which such a curse could be lifted. Thirdly, there was, right up until the advent of the National Health Service in Cornwall, a considerable interest and trade in herbal cures and charms. Those who issued charms and cures were usually not referred to as witches but were, in effect, practising witchcraft. In the public perception, therefore, witches were seen but not publicly proclaimed unless they entered into litigation by default. Lastly, superstition was rife and affected all aspects of the perilous life that many common folk led, both on the land and at sea. The A-Z seeks to fill in the background to the folk mind and places witchcraft in Cornwall into the cultural context which supported it.

ASH TREE

A tree which was sacred to witches. Ash trees were noted for their curative powers, especially against childhood ailments. Hunt witnessed a child being passed through a cleft ash. It was believed that if two parts of the tree were rejoined the child would get well again if he were washed in dew collected from the branches of the tree on three succesive mornings.

If a child was beaten with an ash stick he would stop growing,. Hernia could be cured by crawling through an ash sapling before sunrise and fasting. A rhyme about the ash went as follows:

Even ash, I thee do pluck,
Hoping thus to meet good luck;
If no luck I get from thee,
I shall wish thee on the tree.

BEES

Bees were sacred to the goddess and were venerated by adherents of the Old Religion. In Cornwall they are connected with a number of superstitions connected with death rituals. A swarm of bees seen in May is worth a "yow" (ewe) and it was considered lucky in Cornwall for a swarm to stray near one's house. It was considered very unlucky to sell bees and the inside of the hive was rubed with elderflowers to stop the swarms from leaving them. Honey was taken from the hives on Bartholomew's Day, he being the patron saint of bees. At a meeting of the Penzance Natural History and Antiquarian Society in 1888, a gentleman reported that as a boy he had seen thirty beehives belonging to Joshua Fox of Tregedna tied up in crape because of a death in the family. (M. Courtney, Cornish Feasts and Folklore).

BLIGHT, TAMSIN

Tamsin Blight (otherwise known as "Tammy Blee") was once famous in Helston as a pellar (white witch) and was remembered with affection until the early 1940's by the older people of that town. Tamsin married a man called James Thomas from Illogan who had tried unsuccesfully to make a living as a conjurer. Tamsin left Thomas because a warrant had been issued for his arrest after a complaint made against him by William Paynter following an attempt he had made to remove a spell from his wife. He was described as a "drunken beastly fellow" and was in the habit of removing spells from young men in return for sexual favours. (West Briton newspaper, quoted by Hunt).

According to Bottrell, in her heyday people regularly resorted to Tamsin, especially at the fixed seasons of the year (presumably the eight Celtic or pagan festivals) "to have their protections renewed", while Tamsin herself made regular journeys into the countryside in order to visit those people who were unable to visit her for this purpose.

According to William Paynter (Old Cornwall Society Vol 9, pp 28 - 33), who collected many tales about this famous witch, a woman living near Helston visited Tamsin, complaining that her child was ill and would not respond to medical aid. Tamsin was able to determine the appearance of the woman who had ill-wished the child and she described her in detail. The woman returned home and scratched the arm of the woman (see BLOODING). From that moment onwards, the child began to recover. Another story was reported to Paynter by a resident of Camborne who said that when Tamsin was old and bedridden, people were often brought to her on stretchers and laid at her bedside entirely helpless. They were then healed and able to leave, being in perfect health. Another story tells how when she was very ill, a farmer came and asked her if she would cure his horse. As she was too ill to move, she called her son to her side and touched him, saying a ritual. She then told the farmer that if he could carry her son to where the horse stood, his touch would cure it. He did as he was told and the horse recovered.

BLOODING

According to popular belief, the power of a witch could be broken and her victim released from his spell if she was scratched above the brow until she bled for it was thought that her power lay in her blood and the loss of the blood would therefore mean the loss of her power.

The practice was widespread among "white witches" or pellars in Cornwall right up until the latter part of the 19th Century. In the village of Morvah for example, two old women who lived in the almshouses hardly ever spoke to each other. During the winter one of them fell ill and became convinced that she had been the victim of a spell cast by the other. In order to remove the spell she stuck a rusty nail into her neighbour's arm. The local vicar intervened and threatened to summons the woman if she ever did it again. (Miss Gyles, Old Cornwall Society, Vol 10, p. 4)

On 7 April 1865 Richard Burrows of Creegbrawse was summoned by Elizabeth Evans of Bissoe Pool. Elizabeth claimed to have been attcaked byBurrows who brandished a stick over head saying "I'll take your life." When interviewed by the police Burrows said he thought the woman was a witch and that he had been ill-wished. "I have heard that if you go and bring blood they can never hurt you any more. I was not well in body and mind; and she pretends to do witchcraft, and takes money." He was fined 1s. and costs.

In 1887 a similar case came before the magistrates at Camborne. A young woman whose children were suffering from fever had been told by a neighbour that they had been ill-wished. In order to remove the spell, she vsited a local sorceress. "I have not ill-wished your children," the sorceress protested. "Then I must see your blood," the woman retorted, scratching the other woman on the face until she bled. (Cornish Telegraph, 20 October, 1887)

Witch feeding her familiars, from John Ashton, The Devil In Britain And America, London, 1896.

BURNING ANIMALS

The practice of burning animals was practised in Cornwall as a form of sympathetic magic well into the late 19th Century and is mentiioned by Hunt and other folklorists. The principle seems to have been based on the advice given by "white witches".

Hunt quotes the case of an old Cornish farmer about 1800 who, having suffered a number of disasters, was advised to burn the best calf he possessed. Hunt adds that he has been informed "recently" (1881) of two similar cases. One of them was the sacrifice of a calf by farmer near Portreath, for the purpose of removing a disease which afflicted his sheep and cows. The other was the burning of a live lamb to save his flocks from spells. Hamilton Jenkin ("Cornwall And The Cornish") gives two more examples, both from the Scillies: one from post 1800 when an old mare, supposed to be possessed by an evil sheep-bewitching spirit was burned alive and another in the early part of this century when a famer who had been ill-wished, burnt a chicken alive on the advice of a Penzance wizard to break an evil spell. (The case is reported in the Cornwall Gazette, for 24 April 1802)

The practice of animal burning is mentioned in Frazer's epic study of folklore, The Golden Bough ("Balder The Beautiful, pp. 300 -327). He suggests that in burning the animal the person concerned was burning the witch who is actually incarnate in the animal. "Hence if you burn the creature to ashes you utterly destroy the witch and thereby save the whole of the rest of the flock or herd from her abominable machinations."

The condemnation of this practice was recorded as long ago as 1587 by George Gifford in his pamphlet, "A Dialogue concerning Witches and Witchcraftes". It was sometimes believed that by burning one of the bewitched animals the witch herself would be compelled to appear and then could be dealt with.

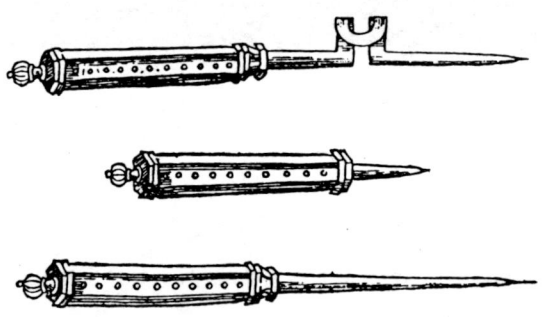

Witch pricking tools

BONFIRES

The tradition of the Baal Fires is one which has survived into the twentieth century. It is linked with the earliest of pagan rituals, that of the Celtic Midsummer Solstice Festival. An early account of the Midsummer fires is given in Hone's Year Book and quoted by Hunt. Hone regarded them as a survival of Druidical practices connected with sun worship but this may not have been the case. Richard Edmonds, an inhabitant of Penzance, recorded celebrations at Penzance when torches werelit on Midsummer's Eve and bonfires lit ("The Lands End District"). On this eve a line of tar barrels adorned the streets of Penz ance and young people used to pass up and down the streeet swinging torches made of heavy canvas steeped in tar.

That the tradition is an ancient one is without doubt. An observer writing in the Gentlemen's Magazine as long ago as 1795 records "the people of all ages dancing around the fires until until a late hour of the night, swinging their children through the flames, not in such manner as to hurt them, though sometimes to singe their clothes."

At St Just miners would bore rows of holes in rock, fill them with gunpowder and then explode them on this eve. At the close of the celebrations in Penzance people, would jump through the flames of the bonfires, bleieving that any one who did so would be preserved from evil through the coming year.

A similar festival was held in Polperro on the Feast of St Peter, held on the 10th of July. On this night young fishermen set fire to a pile of faggots and tar barrels built on the beach, then dancearound it.
Until 1828 a bonfire was held on Midsummer Day on the small island off Mousehole and men and women crossed over from the village for the occasion. (Old Cornwall Society, Summer 1932, p.11)

The fire festivals of Cornwall are a living survival of the witchcraft tradition. Midsummer was called Goluan in Cornish and according to Dr Borlase, who first noted these festivals, signified Light and Rejoicing. The correct translation appears to be "gol-Yowan", the feast or wake of John, because it is held on St John's Eve, 23rd of June. In fact the early Christian church celebrated the Saint's festival on this eve in order to absorb the existing pagan tradition. The word "Baal Fire" is derived from the Celtic Beltane. There is clearly a confusion between May day and Midsummer Day by early commentators and they assumed that the midsummer fires were in honour of the god Bel, a traditional British deity. In fact bonfires in May are not known in Cornwall.

Various theories have been put forward to explain the lighting of the midsummer bonfires and of the ritual of leaping through them. According to Frazer ("The Golden Bouigh"), the fires were originally intended to mimic the sun as the source of life. The ritual was a form of sympathetic magic. According to another theory it served as a protection against witchcraft, but this is clearly a later development. It is significant that the two chief fire festivals of Europe occur at the times of the solstices, those very times when the sun was about to sink into a slow decline.

BURNING THE WITCH

A game called "Burning the witch" was once played in Cornwall. It is mentioned by Borlasein his "Traditions and Hearthside Stories of West Cornwall". According to the folklorist, "To play the game .... a pole about five feet long, such as a pike- staff or shovel-hilt is placed with each end resting on a low stool. A lighted candle is placed on the floor at a short distance from the pole, on which the person who undertakes to burn the witch endeavours to keep sitting, with the feet also crossed (at the ankles) resting on the pole clear of any other support or help, except a stick about five feet in length. In a slit at the end of this stick is placed the paper, or rag figure, to represent the witch to be burnt for fun, by the person sitting in this ticklish position, who often falls many times before the paper figure can be burnt at the candle on the floor."

The game is a grim reminder of the time when witches were tortured and then burned. In England this was not permitted by law but it was in Scotland and on the Continent.

Frontispiece to Matthew Hopkins' Discovery of Witches, London, 1647, showing witches and their familiars.

Scold's bridle, used as a punishment
for troublesome women. A version of
this type of torture instrument was once
held by the Penzance Town Council.
Photo: The author, courtesy, Graham
King, Museum of Witchcraft.

Charms were often a form of sympathetic magic designed to cure the sick. The word "charm" comes from the Old English "cyrm" meaning a song or hymn. Many of the oldest recorded charms have a Christian bias and exist as ritual forms of words. Roughly they can be divided into two types: those intended to heal or cure disease and love charms. Although our records of witchcraft ritual are scarce, especially in Cornwall, we have an abundance of charms which survived into the late 19th Century and many of these were recorded. Some, like wart charming, are still practised quite widely.

Among the commonest of charms were those cast for thrush, deafness, warts, sore eyes, shingles and epilepsy. Whooping cough can be be cured by filling a muslin bag with spiders and hanging it round the neck of thevictim, while styes on the eye are cured by touching them with a cat's tail.

Margaret Courtney (Cornish Feasts And Folklore) records a number of charms common in the last century among Cornish people. Several of these reveal in their rituals the symbolic connection withthe belief in the Goddess. For example, diseases could be cured by taking three burning sticks from the hearth of the overlooker and making the patient pass over them three times before extinguishing them with water. Another charm involves placing nine bramble leaves in a basin of holy well water and passing the leaves over the diseased part, quoting the verse: "Three virgins came from the east, one brought fire, the others brought frost. Out fire ! In frost ! In the name of the Father, Son and Holy Ghost." Again, she recalls an old Cornishman who lived in West Cornwall. He charmed warts, cataracts and other conditions by spitting three times on the afflicted part, then saying: "in the name of the Father, Son and Holy Ghost I bid thee begone." Again, the condition known as "kennels" (ulcerated eyes) was cured by uttering the three virgins rhyme nine times. The moon (sacred to witches) is also invoked in several charms.To cure diseases, hands were washed in a basin in the moon's rays, the words being uttered: "I wash my hands in this thy dish, /Oh man in the moon, do grant my wish/ And come and take away this." The moon also was invoked for the curing of corns. The symbolism of THREE and NINE is widespread and although overlaid with Christian allegory, a clear reference to the Old Religion and goddess worship. Hunt quotes a charm for whooping cough which involves passing a child naked NINE times over the back and under the belly of a female donkey. Three spoonfuls of milk are then taken from the teats of the animal, three hairs from its back and three from its belly. The child must then stand in the milk for three hours and be given the medicine in three doses, repeated on three mornings. A cure for warts (Hamilton-Jenkin) mentions taking a pod containing NINE peas, selecting the ninth and throwing it away with the words: "Wart, wart, dry away." As the pea rots so the wart disappears.

In fact the folk use of Christian imagery in charms reveals how the Cornish wove pagan magical ritual into the "official" teachings of the Church in order to achieve practical effects when curing diseases. A sovereign remedy for hiccups for example, was to take a stale piece of Good Friday bun and grate it into a glass of water. This is then hung in the kitchen. Another example of this fusion of beliefs is the charm for eye diseases. On the third day of the moon, when the crescent shape is seen, a knife is shown prior to cutting club moss and the words uttered: "As Christ healed theissue of blood,/ So I bid you begone;/ in the name of ... etc." The club moss must be cut at sun down and the practitioner must kneel. The club moss must then be mixed with butter and made into an ointment.

CHARMERS

In Cornwall, the great majority of reported witches were female and of these most were what people regarded as "White" witches. The most common of all the white witches were the charmers or healers. Right up until the late 19th Century it was common for women to take their children to a doctor's surgery and announce that they had already had the illnesses "charmed". The word CHARM comes from the Old English CYRM, meaning a hymn or choral song and this in turn is derived from the Latin CARMEN, meaning a sacred incantation to the Goddess Carmenta, inventor of the words of power. The word CHARM therefore once represented men's belief that women could gain the assistance of the Goddess through their power of words. The word "enchant" came from incantare, meaning to "sing over."

Charming has an ancient pedigree. In fact the Anglo Saxon Leechbook provides a number of charms which are invocations to the goddess with a Christian overlay. According to Hunt people in the parish of Zennor possessed the power to charm in an astonishing degree and they could stop blood from flowing, however freely it ran just by thinking of a charm. However, a man or woman would not communicate their charms freely to members of the opposite sex. People would travel miles to have themselves or their children cured of "wildfires" (erysipelas), ringworm or pain in the limbs or in the teeth or kennels (ulcerations) on the eyes. A woman wholived at Zennor told a correspondent of Hunt's that there were three charmers in the area: one at New Mill, one at Morvah and herself. Her charm for stopping blood had a Christian overlay, as many charms did:

"Christ was born in Bethlehem;
Baptized in the river Jordan.
The river stood -
So shall thy blood,
Mary Jane Polgrain (or whatever the person may be called),
In the name of the Father &c."

Magical medicine, which was once the only kind available to country folk in Cornwall, provided remedies right up until the outbreak of the First World War and many of these remedies have in fact been found to be based on commonsense. (Urine, for example, an integral element in many rituals of healing, has genuine curative properties.)

In a letter written to the folklorist, Robert Hunt, the correspondent mentions several instances of charming which had proved to be extremely effective. A renowned charmer at Redruth, one Thomas Martin, was said to have cured children of fits and adults of their deformities. Also in Falmouth the same correspondent writes of an aged woman who was able to cure the affliction known as "kennel" (erysipelas). A young woman was once sent to the charmer's house. When she arrived she declared that she did not believe in the charmer's abilities. The old woman then asked her to describe the symptoms of her father's condition. She then went upstairs for half an hour and returned, taking no money and asking the young woman to return home. The father was then cured. In another case a man afflicted by severe cramp sent his wife to charmer who advised him to place his slippers with the toes turned upwards at the foot of the bed. This he did and he gained relief from the cramp. Then one night he was badly afflicted. On awakening he observed that he had placed his slippers in the opposite direction. He then returned them to the correct position and the pain visited him no more.

Wart charming has survived until this day and of this there are many variant forms. One is to rub the wart on a snail which is then impaled on a thorn. It is believed that as the snail dies so does the wart. Another is to rub the wart on a piece of meat which is then thrown away or buried and as the meat rots so will the wart. A chalk mark can also be drawn inside a chimney and as it fades so the wart withers away. Michael Williams in his Supernatural In Cornwall (Bossiney Books) records an interview with one Charlie Bennett who lived in Tintagel. Charlie simply asks for the subject's name and age and then utters a form of words (again with a Christian overlay). He charms ring worm in human beings, cattle and horses. Like many charmers, Charlie had the tradition in his family and inherited a form of words which had been committed to paper.

Hunt also records a cure for warts reported to him by the vicar of Bodmin, consisting of a bottle of pins laid in a newly made grave. Each wart was touched with a new pin and the pin then dropped into the bottle. As the pins rusted so the warts decayed.

Another favourite Cornish charm involved using knots - a familiar aspect of the Old Craft. A method of stopping a nose bleed, for example, was to knot a red cord. The red symbolized blood and the knot a clot. For warts, a piece of string would be taken and as many knots tied on it as there are warts on the body of the victim. Each wart would then be carefully touched with the knot dedicated to it. The string would then be buried and the wart would fade away as the string decayed. Also to touch each wart with a pebble, to place the pebbles in a bag and to lose the bag on the way to church was a favourite remedy. Hunt recalls as a child having a large wart on one of his fingers. He was taken to an elderly woman in Gwinear. Two charred sticks were taken from the fire on the hearth and crossed over the wart, words being uttered by the charmer. The wart then disappeared. (also see CHARMS)

CORN DOLLIES

The corn dolly was known in Cornwall as the "Pedn Yar" or chicken's head. This was named after the image of the harvest goddess which was fashioned from the neck of the corn or last sheaf, cut at harvest time. (See CRYING THE NECK) In Cornwall, the corn dolly was often given to the best milk cow or the bull of the farm.

Bearded wheat was used to make the dolly and this type of wheat had a high nutrional value. The corn dollies varied in design from region to region. According to Jan Gendall ("Corn Dollies - A Pagan Origin", Meyn Mamvro, No. 4), those from St Neot were shoulder high, while others were much smaller like the button hole love tokens from Indian Queens.

Sabine Baring Gould, the west Country folklorist, in "Book of Cornwall", makes reference to harvest love rituals and quotes a contemporary Quaker who questioned the validity of "making sweet hay with the maidens". Clearly corn dollies were given as love tokens between lovers. Since they were also given to cattle and ploughed into the ground it can be seen that they were once regarded as powerful sources of fertility by followers of the Old Religion.

CRYING THE NECK

The ceremony of "crying the neck" is a harvest ritual which is one of the few remaining pagan rituals left in Cornwall. Although it died a death with the advent of the mechanical reaper, it was revived at Towednack in the summer of 1928 by the Old Cornwall Society and has continued ever since, although, very regrettably, in a Christianized format.

At harvest time, when the corn was cut, one sheaf of corn was left for the ritual, in which both men and women took part. It was a tradition that the oldest reaper would cut this sheaf, crying: " I hav'et ! I hav'et ! I hav'et !" The others then reply: "What have'ee ? What have'ee ? What have'ee ?" He then replies: "A neck ! A neck ! A neck !" Three loud cheers follow, then the neck is cut, made into a miniature sheaf, decorated with ribbons and flowers and carried home and hung up on a beam in the kitchen where it is left to the next harvest. Hunt recalls that there was a game in which a young man would attempt to get the neck into the farm house past a dairy maid who guarded the door, bearing a pail of water. If he failed, the pail would be emptied over his head.

Frazer in the Golden Bough describes the ritual in some detail, explaining the "neck" as the "corn spirit", herein conceived in human or animal form. The last standing corn is part of its body - the neck, its head or tail. In support of this, we know that in the parish of St Buryan the neck was known in Cornish as "pedn-yar" (hen's head).

In fact Crying the Neck is a variant form of a ritual of propitiation to the Corn Goddess and was originally carried out at Lughnasadh. As the Corn Mother, the Neck (and often the last reaper as well) are known as "The Old Grandmother" in East Prussia, the Cailleach or Witch in Scotland and in Pembrokeshire the Gwrach, usually translated as "Hag" but more correctly "Crone". In fact this last word, the Welsh Gwrach, or Cornish Gwragh is often found in place names in combinations such as Crows An Wra (the Witch's Cross, near Sennen). The word "crow" has various dialect pronunciations in West Cornwall and Graw and Graa are common among older people. The Corn Spirit was therefore the Corn Mother.

CUNNING MAN

Another name for a pellar or white witch, The Cunning Man fulfilled a particular role in that he was employed to remove the spells cast by witches. The spells he used were invariably Christian ones and he (The Cunning Man was always masculine) was frequently a feared member of the community.

The Cornish Cunning Men flourished right into the latter part of the nineteenth century and beyond. They were employed to recover lost and stolen property, sold love philtres and countered the evil eye. Hunt tells of how the Wise Man of Illogan persuaded a sea captain, who thought he was under the spell of a witch, to follow him to a beach at Hayle for an experiment in counter witchcraft. Having taken his fee, the Cunning Man began to chant and then threw a stone into the sea. This, he assured the sea captain, transferred the spell to himself. The Cunning Man then left, bent double. Hunt also recounts a tale about a Cunning Man who visited a mental asylum hoping to cure an imbecile girl there. He showed his visiting card which bore the letters MA. When questioned about this he replied that this meant Master of the Black Arts. An attempt was made to prosecute him under the Witchcraft Act but this broke down. There was also a powerful Cunning Man who lived in Nanstallan, near Bodmin (Hunt). Thomas ..... removed spells from people and cattle but because of his succes he was waylaid and robbed and forced to move to Fowey. According to Hunt, "The White Witch was supposed to possess the higher power of removing the spell, and of punishing the individual by whose wickedness the wrong had been inflicted." (Also see PELLERS and WHITE WITCHES)

DEAD MAN'S HAND

A dead man's hand was thought to have curative properties, especially that of a hanged man. Margaret Courtney mentions several instances of this tradition in Cornwall. It was known as a cure for eye complaints and even facial disfigurements. One correspondent recalls having suffered from a disfigurement on his upper lip. He was taken as a child to a house in Causeway Head, Penzance and there the deceased owner of the house had his hand passed over the boy's lip. By slow degrees the disfigurement disappeared. There was, apparently, no virtue in the hand of a dead relation.

Severed hands occur in many places in Britain. In a Roman Catholic Church in Ashton-in-Makerfield, for example, there is the preserved hand of a dead man which purports to have great curative values. It belonged to Father Edmund Arrowsmith who was executed in Lancaster in 1628 for being a Catholic. After he was executed the hand was severed and kept.

DELABOLE, WITCH OF

According to William Paynter, (OCS, Vol 9, p. 28 - 33) there was a renowned witch who lived in Delabole, called "Old Ann". She was consulted for her healing abilities by many people who lived in the district, including an old woman from Trewarmett, who suffered from a sore leg. Old Ann used a charmed handkerchief which had to be placed on the affected spot from above downwards, striking it towards the toes. The evil would then ooze out from the feet. A woman from Tintagel who suffered from severe shingles, also wished to visit Old Ann but was unable to do so. She sent an aunt instead who took with her three handkerchiefs. One of these Ann charmed by putting her hand on it and uttering an incantation. By the time she arrived back at her'niece's village, the latter had already improved her condition.

EPILEPSY

Epilepsy was once more common than it is now. Cures and charms against epilepsy, based on the craft of the Old Religion, were practised widely in the last century in Cornwall. Money was collected at the church door by the afflicted person from a member of the opposite sex and changed for sacrament money (silver) which was then made into a ring to be worn day and night (Courtney). Another custom was for the afflicted party to walk three times round a church at midnight, then to stand at the altar. These customs originate from the middle ages when the building of a church would be regarded in much the same way as a more ancient site. The ring that offered protection was seen as a way by which the wearer could gain magical power from those who had entered into a holy space. Another, more ancient cure for epilepsy which can be traced to wiccan origins is the placing of a toad's legs into a bag which would then be worn around the sufferer's neck. A man from Camborne was cured of epileptic fits using this method (Cornishman, December 1881).

EYE DISEASES

In an age where opticians and doctors were scarce, people in Cornwall relied on the wise woman to cure them of eye disease. Many of the cures used were accompanied by ritual sayings, some of which were apparent interpretations of Christian ritual. Courtney relates how a correspondent recalled an old man who lived in West Cornwall. He made a good income by charming warts and cataracts. He would spit three times and breathe three times on the afflicted part, muttering: "In the name of the Father, Son and Holy Ghost I bid thee begone." For cataracts he would collect the small white dew snail with a hawthorn spine and let a drop of the liquid fall onto the afflicted eye. This was accompanied by an ointment made from house leeks and raw cream.

FAIRIES

Fairies were once part of the folk imagination in Cornwall and as such were treated with respect by followers of the Old Religion. (See ANN JEFFERIES, for example) It is possible that the "little people" were once the neolithic people who, as they retreated into more remote places in Cornwall, became mythologised and were then regarded as the people of the underworld. There are many tales about fairies and "spriggans" in Cornwall.

Fairies were thought to have haunted the ancient sites in the county and were believed to bring bad luck to those who destroyed them. When unmolested, fairies bring good fortune to places they frequent but they were thought to be spiteful if interfered with. They would frequently spirit people away to fairyland where their subjects would be entranced. They might then be found wandering the moors, having fallen into a deep sleep. There is a story in St Allen (near Truro) of a boy who went for a walk one evening near a wood in order to gather flowers. Hearing sweet music he went into some undergrowth. Here he fell asleep and was conveyed to fairyland where he saw pillars of glass supporting great arches. (Spriggans were thought to guard vast treasures buried underground). Many days passed before he was then rediscovered.

It was once a custom in East Cornwall to leave holes in the walls when houses were being built so that the fairies could enter and leave at their own will; to stop them from so doing was to invited bad luck. Country people in East Cornwall also put a prayer book under their children's pillows to keep away piskies. The piskies controlled the mists and could cast a thick veil over a traveller.

Fairies could also be responsible for changelings. A poor woman at Launceston was once convinced that her child had been taken away and a fairy child substituted. Hunt believed that people suffering from scrofula were often mistaken for changelings because of their pale countenances and flushed cheeks. The spriggans (probably mythological descendants of the Scandinavian invaders) are to be found only in cairns or barrows and some thought them to be the ghosts of giants.

The Bucca was the name of a spirit that it was thought necessary to propitiate. At harvest a piece of bread was thrown over the left shoulder to ensure good luck. (See CRYING THE NECK) The Bucca or Puck was probably a taboo substitute for a god. At Newlyn in the last century pilchards were thrown over the left shoulder onto the shore in order to secure a good catch. It is likely that Bucca replaced a much older god of the woodland and harvest which may have been the male consort of the goddess.

FLORA DAY

The Christianized (and mistaken) name for the Helston Furry Day. It also goes by the name of Faddy. This is an ancient pagan (Beltane) custom which was originally celebrated on May 1st but later was changed to 8th of May to coincide with the feast of St Michael, whose legend of devil rousting was connected with Helston. The purpose of the Furry Dance was to bring in "the summer and the may-o", as the song suggests. The name Flora derives from the Roman Floralia but the confusion dates from the 18th Century when the rituals of the Furry were classicized. The word "furry" is Cornish for the English equivalent "gol" meaning a feast or holiday. Edward Lhuyd, who visited Cornwall in 1700 refers to the parish feast of Illogan (near Redruth) as a "Furri day", so it would seem that such feast days were popular across Cornwall. It is significant that at the Lizard and Penryn the furry days were celebrated on the 1st and 3rd of May, the old date for Beltane (Hitchens & Drew, History of Cornwall, 1824). The pre- Christian element of the day, known as the Hal An Tow, still points to its pagan origins (see HAL AN TOW), as does the tradition of spring cleaning the house and greening the streets. The Furry dance itself is performed in a spiral fashion and dancers wind their way in and out of local houses. The serpentine nature of the dance also confirms its ancient, pre-Christian origins.

FRADDAM, WITCH OF

Reported to be the most powerful witch in the west country, the witch of Fraddam was thwarted many times by the Lord of Pengerswick, a white witch and sorcerer (Hunt). It was said that she took herself to Kynance Cove and there raised the devil by incantations. She pledged her soul to him for the aid he promised her. Lord Pengerswick got the better of this sorceress and imprisoned her in a coffin which he hurled into the air, crying "There she is settled until the day of doom". The Witch of Fraddam still floats up and down over the seas and around the coast in her coffin. She still works her mischief, stirring up the sea with her ladle and broom until the waves swell into mountains.

GUISE DANCING

Guise dancing was once a common custom · in Cornwall and served part of a pagan midwinter festival. It was carried out between Christmas Day and Twelfth Night and was adhered to by bands of young people in both Penzance and St Ives. Cross dressing was involved as was the performace of a mummer's play, 'usually ˪ that of St George and the Dragon. A writer describing guise dancing in PEnzance in 1831 likened it to an Italian Carnival, so richly attired were the participants. It was also popular on the Scilly Isles and is mentioned in 1750 by Robert Heath. The word guise means "to go mumming" and our word "geezer" means "an old guise dancer", i.e. a strangely dressed person.

The origins of guise dancing go back to pre-Christian times and the mumming play which was once the central attraction features St George and The Dragon, familiar figures in the medieval miracle plays. The resurrection of one of the characters, the Turkish Knight, indicates that we are here dealing with a fertility ritual, aimed at restoring the failing powers of the midwinter sun. As such, guise dancing is an ancient survival of the Old Religion.

HAL-AN-TOW

The Hal-An-Tow is the most ancient part of the Helston Furry Dance and was revived in 1930, after having fallen into disuse, following the Furry's Christianization. It comprises an ancient song which lists Robin Hood, Spaniards and St George and this accompanies a mumming play. The Hal-An-Tow is performed in the early part of the celebrations by members of the Old Cornwall Society and senior pupils of Helston School. The Hal-An-Tow is certainly pre-17th Century and may go back earlier. It could have been part of the ancient May rituals which comprised the King and Queen of May, the Morris Dance and the Hobby Horse. The words of the song are similar to the older versions of the Padstow Obby Oss (see OBBY OSS).

Although some think that the words Hal-An-Tow are synonymous with "heel and toe", it is unlikely that this is so. A 17th Century Cornish writer believes the phrase is close to "Haile-an-Taw". "Hal" or "hayl" is a Cornish word for moorland while "Taw" means houses. The phrase could therefore be translated as "in the town and the country". The next part of the line, "Jolly rumble -o" would mean: there will be merrymaking. The figure of "Aunt Mary Moses" who appears in the song is similar to "Aunt Ursula Birdhood" who appears in the Obby Oss song. She appears to be a form of the Crone, the final form of the goddess who relates to the dark moon and the resting earth who must be revived by the May festivities.

HALLOWEEN

The old Celtic festival of Samhain, the beginning of the Celtic year and a time when the veil between the living and the dead was thinnest. At such times divination was practised. This festival of the Old Religion was widely upheld in Cornwall, which had its own rituals.

The old name for Halloween is Allantide, a corruption of the Middle English, Alhalwen-tyd. The name is etymologically linked with Avallen, the Cornish for an apple tree and it is no coincidence that the Cornish used apples for divination. The village of St Allen, near Truro, may also derive its name from this word.

The sacred hare, symbol of the witch.
A large ceramic statue found buried in
a caravan park in West Cornwall. Photo:
The author, Courtesy: Graham King,
Museum of Witchcraft.

Most of the customs connected to Halloween which have been recorded by folklorists are connected with fertility and marriage. There is also a connection with sacred places. In St Cubert's parish, East Cornwall, is a Holy well. It was named after its healing powers had been discovered on All Hallows Day.

Many charms were attempted on Halloween when young women would attempt to discover the names of their future husbands. These included pouring melted lead through the handle of the front door key and scrying the shapes that resulted from this. Another custom included rolling three names, each written onto a piece of paper and screwing them into a ball. These were dropped into a basin of water and the one which came to the surface would betoken the name of the intended one. A wedding ring would also be suspended from a piece of cotton and held between finger and thumb while the words were uttered: "If my husband's name is to be ... let this ring swing !" An apple pip flicked into the air suggested the direction of the intended lover's home, the words being uttered: "north, south, east west,/ Tell me where my love does rest."

The far western town of St Just In Penwith kept the revelries connected with the Old religion right up until the heyday of the mining industry. The feast day therewas held on the nearest Sunday to All Saint's Day. Games were played on the Monday like Kook, a quoit throwing competition, wrestling and keels or ninepins.

HARE

The hare has for long been regarded as a sacred and taboo creature. It was also regarded as one of the forms which a witch assumed when shape-shifting. There are several taboos connected with the hare. A white hare often spelt disaster. It was the death token at Wheal Vor: the wife of the sorcerer turned into a hare; maidens who were betrayed often turned into hares and haunted their lovers and it was believed that white hares could only be killed with a silver bullet (like werewolves). The legendary huntsman Wild Harris of Kenegie (near Gulval, Penzance) was killed when hunting by a fall from his horse when it was frightened by a white hare, the spirit of a deserted maiden, which crossed his path.

There are many tales of a hare who pursued hounds and, when shot by a silver bullet, then transformed itself into the figure of a local witch. Deane and Shaw recall a case which took place in 1934. A family went on a motoring holiday in north Cornwall and went for a walk on the moors. They came across a large hare sitting on its haunches and shrieking. One of the family picked up the hare and calmed it, whereupon the animal hopped away. When they returned to the hotel they told the landlord their story. The landlord turned pale and told the family he could no longer accommodate them. They duly complained and the landlord changed his mind. Nevertheless, their stay was made uncomfortable and when they finally did leave they were told that nobody but a witch would handle a hare as they had done.

HARRIS, JENNY

A reputed witch who is described by Hunt as "poor, old, and from the world's ill-usage, rendered malicious". She was often accused of casting evil spells which fell on cattle, children, men and women. A washerwoman who believed that she was under Jenny's spell, attacked her, scratching her arm and gouging it from the elbow to the wrist. (This was an ancient practice known as blooding. It was believed that through such an attack the power of the witch would be broken.) The attack came to the notice of local magistrates who fined the attacker five pounds.

HERBS

The village wise woman, witch or herbalist was once the sole administrator of medicines. Male medicine arrived relatively late in Cornwall and was slow at making inroads in the area of healing. Even in the 19th Century old people were believers in the adage that "there is a doctor in every hedge" (Hamilton-Jenkin). In 1826 Polwhele wrote that the "church-town crony will sometimes cure a disease which has been given up by her betters as irremediable." The Cornish believed in the power of herbal remedies and were prepared to travel for miles to visit a wise woman. Herbal remedies were once legion in the county. For example, adder wounds were cured by a concoction of plantain and sallad oil. Colds in the head were cured by an infusion of mugwort while elderflower was used to cure fevers (scaw blowth in Cornish). Camomile tea was used to help stomach ache and elder and camomile was adminstered as a purgative. Mallow was made into an ointment and applied to inflammations; coltsfoot was smoked as a precaution against lung disease; earache was treated by cooked onion used as a compress while "bullorns" (snails) were used in a poultice to draw poison from infected wounds. Many herbs were used in connection with the phases of the moon. clubmoss was used for eye diseases and thought effective if cut on the third day of the moon and the knife for cutting the moss had to be shown to the moon while a charm was uttered. Some cures originated from the fear of witchcraft. Ash was often carried in the form of a stick to ward off adders and to disempower a witch.

The deep-rooted belief in the power and efficacy of herbs survived in Cornwall, despite the attempts of the Church and the established patriarchy to demonize witchcraft lore. A blacksmith, one Ralph Barnes, cured himself of cancer by ingesting large amounts of hemlock. (1790) In a number of parishes clergymen practised herbalism and simple folk magic in addition to performing their Christian duties (Deane & Shaw). Hugh Atwell, Rector of Ewe (1559 - 1615) was an example of this longstanding tradition and apparently was not criticised by the Bishop of Exeter for so doing.

ILL- WISHING

It was a tradition in Cornwall that when anything unforeseen happened, especially to farmers' livestock, this would be put down to "ill wishing". The aggrieved person would then consult a pellar (see PELLER) in order to have the curse removed. The methods by which such a curse could be removed varied. Sometimes a heart of a sheep or bullock was stuck full of pins and then roasted over an open fire.This would be accompanied by the ritual words:

It is not this heart I wish to burn,
But the person's heart I wish to turn,
Wishing them neither rest nor peace
Till they are dead and gone.

Sometimes a photograph would substituted. (OCS Second Series, Vol 11, 21.) A common expression used in Cornwall is " 'E me 'andsome, you're looking brer ill-wished." The phrase is an intriguing survival from memories of the old fear of the power of the witch. Hamilton Jenkin tells a story about a poor labourer who rented a cottage from a farmer in the south coast of Cornwall. He owned a dog who attacked the farmer's sheep. One day the labourer took his dog to the river in readiness to drown the dog. He went on board a barge and there began to swear and curse about the farmer. To an audience of bargees he cursed the farmer's stock and crops. Then he threw the dog into the water and let it drown. From that time onwards the farmer received nothing but ill luck. Courtney relates a story about a farmer in West Cornwall whose cows were dying of indigestion. He was instructed to visit a pellar in Exeter. There he was given instructions to return home and, on nearing his farm, he would see an old woman in a field hoeing turnips. This woman would be the originator of the evil eye. He was told to tear off some of her dress and burn it with some of the hair from the tails of his surviving stock. He carried out these instructions and lost no more stock. Another farmer suffering similar loss of stock was told by the Exeter pellar to bring home some bottles of elixir and make an image out of dough. This he pierced from the nape of the neck downward in the line of the spine with a large blanket pin. The dough and the pin were then burned in a fire of hazel and ash wood in order to increase the agonies of the witch. The cure failed.

Accusations of ill- wishing continued right through the 19th Century. Deane and Shaw recall the case of three women called De Freez who in July 1845 attacked a woman called Warne because they feared they had been ill- wished by her. Another case involved a man from Ludgvan who had kept his wife on bread and water as a punishment for her sister who had ill-wished him and as a means of removing the curse.. A case at Port Quinn, near Port Isaac (North Cornwall) concerned an old woman called Mollie W. who lived about 90 years ago in a ruined cottage. She was known locally as "an evil woman." One day a neighbour's pigs crossed her clean doorstep. She shouted that they should never cross port Quin again alive (their sty being on the other side of the bridge). Within a few hours the pigs were dead. Old Mollie also bewitched the cattle of a Mr T. In order to break the spell, Mrs T. burned the heart of an animal which she had stuck with pins. The daughter of Mrs T. recalled how the very next day the old woman visited their house, this being a condition of the spell breaking, that the caster of the spell is forced to appear to the victim before she can be at peace again. (OCS Vol 4, p.289) An interesting case was reported in the Penzance Gazette for 20 May 1840. A mackerel boat called the Broom was thought to be cursed and as a consequence, caught no fish. The cause was attributed to a young woman in Newlyn West. The remedy was to burn a portion of the boat's nets in public.

The high incidence of accusations of ill wishing is an interesting phenomenon. Prior to the major anti-witch legislation of the 17th Century we find few cases of ill-wishing. As women began to be feared for the power that they held, cases of ill-wishing began to be the norm and any woman, whether young or old, could be accused, even if she were clearly innocent. The most likely women were those who were likely to be outspoken or independent by nature. The tradition of ill-wishing in Cornwall can therefore be seen as an inevitable outcome of the mysogny of the witchcraft hunt.

A witch brewing up a storm. From Olaus Magnus, Historia de gentibus septentrionalibus, Rome, 1555.

JAR, WITCH

Witch jars were devices used to act as a protection against an ill wisher. The blood of a bewitched person, combined with urine, hair and nail clippings was stoppered in a bottle and placed over a fire. This caused the ill wisher to burn or writhe in torment. In the trial of Jane Wenham of Walkerne, Hertfordshire, proof that she had bewitched a servant girl was obtained by providing a witch bottle containing urine, hair and nail clippings. This was placed on a fire and burst. She then suffered relief for the first time. The bottles were often placed in chimnies to prevent the witch from entering the house and causing further harm. One such bottle was found in the chimney of a house in Padstow in 1935. The custom is probably linked to the idea of propitiation . There have been several cases of rats being buried beneath the walls of houses, for example, in Cornwall, and bottles containing coins.

' JEFFERIES, ANNE

Anne Jefferies was born in St Teath, North Cornwall, in December 1626. She was a remarkable healer and clairvoyant and one of many women in Cornwall who were made the subject of systematic persecution by the 17th Century patriarchy, not least for her political views. She gained considerable notoriety in Cornwall for her ability to converse with fairies and although a Christian retained many of the powers thought by the Church to be associated with the Old Religion, Witchcraft..

A full account of her unusual life was contained in a document published by Moses Pitt, a London publisher (subsequently republished by S. Baring Gould in his Cornish Characters And Strange Events) Pitt asked his nephew, a lawyer, to interview Anne about her life since she had been unjustly imprisoned by the notorious magistrate Tregeagle. In September 1691 he wrote a letter to Pitt telling him that his sister's husband, one Humphry Martyn, had interviewed Anne who was reluctant to talk about her experiences.

Anne was a poor man's child from the parish and was sent to live with the Martyn family, working for them as a servant. In the year 1645 when she was 19 years old she claimed that she was visited by six "persons of small stature, all clothed in green, which she called fairies." Anne promptly fell into a fit and was taken into the house by the family. When she was subsequently put to bed she called out to them: "They are just gone out of the window ! Do you not see them ?"

Martyn went on to relate how Anne, being weak, was locked into the house while Martyn's mother walked to the local mill. On her way home she fell and broke her leg and was eventually discovered by a neighbour. Anne greeted her and showed that she already knew of the fall, asking her if she might heal the leg by stroking it. This the mother consented to and the leg healed quickly. She then revealed that she had been told of her mistress's fall by the fairies. She went on to say that they always appeared in even numbers: 2, 4, 6 or 8.

Anne's fame soon spread to Land's End and even London. Many people came to be cured by her but she would take no reward for her services. She refrained from eating food provided for her by the Martyn family, saying that the fairy folk gave her food. On one occasion Martyn's son knocked on her bedroom door and was invited in but on entering could see no one.

Eventually Anne's reputation was such that she was considered a danger by the local Christian minister and she was examined by priests and a local magistrate. She gave them rational answers and told them that she was telling them the truth. The ministers "endeavouring to persuade her they were evil spirits resorted to her and that it was the delusions of the devil. But how could that be when she did no hurt, but good to all who came to her... ?

After the magistrate and the priests had left her, Anne was again visited by the fairies who told her to "desire them to read in the 1st Epistle of S. John ... "Dearly beloved, believe not every spirit, but try the spirits whether they be of God." The quote was then found in the Bible by Anne and Martyn then makes the point that Anne was illiterate.

John Tregeagle, the local J.P. sent a warrant for Anne's arrest and she was then sent to Bodmin gaol. In fact Anne had been told of her imminent arrest prior to the warrant being served and had asked the fairies if she should hide. They answered no but to go with the constable. The Martyns were subsequently asked to give evidence. Anne was discharged from prison but for a while was kept a prisoner by Tregeagle himself who refused to feed her. After being released from prison she was sent to live with Martyn's sister, a widow who lived near Padstow. She continued to practise healing and in the course of time married.

There is an interesting rider to the story. Some time in the 1930's the author Hamilton Jenkin (Cornwall And Its People) came across some MSS in the Bodleian Library, dated February and April 1647. The writer of the MSS stated: "I can acquaint you with ... news ... of a young girle which foretells things to come and most have fallen out true. She eats nothing but sweetmeats, as Alemans (almonds) comfited and the like, which are brought her by small people cladd in greene and sometimes by birds. She cures most diseases, the Falling sickness especially and broken bones, only with the touch of her hands.... She hath been examined by three able Divines, and gives a good accompt of her religion and hath the Scriptures very perfectly, though quite unlearned. They are fearful to meddle with her for she tells them to their faces that none of them are able to hurt her... At present she is at Bodmin, at the Mayor's house ... She says the King shall enjoy his own and be revenged of his enemies."

Anne's long imprisonment had much to do, it seems, not with her belief in fairies but with her political views. As so often in witchcraft cases politics and faith were inextricably intertwined in cases of persecution.

KIMBLY CAKE

A piece of cake or sometimes bread which was given at weddings and christenings as a way of warding off the evil eye. When the party leave the church the cake is given to the first person who appears. Quiller-Couch mentions the custom as does William Pengelly (Western Morning News, quoted by Courtney). The cake was about the size of a tea plate and contained currants and saffron.

KENIDZHEK (KENIDJACK) WITCH

Hunt tells a story of a witch who was the guardian of a holy well near the "Gump" near Kenidjack, (St Just area). Two miners lived not far from the well with their sister. They warned her not to go to the well after daylight. One Saturday night, however, she forgot their warning and went to the well. She saw an old woman sitting near the well in a red shawl (red is a witch's traditional colour). She asked her what she wanted there at that time of the night but received no reply. The young woman plunged her pitcher into the well but it brought up no water. She repeated the process but met with no success. She then became frightened and left the well. When she returned home she told her brothers what had happened and they told her that she had seen the ghost of Old Moll, a witch who had been a great terror in her lifetime and who had cast many fearful spells on them. The story is an interesting one since it demonstrates how supernatural guardians were assigned to wells and that they were always female and followers of the Old Religion. The young woman is told not to visit the well since her brothers fear the ancient powers it holds - feminine powers. When she does visit the well she is unable to draw up water since the well has become taboo. It is a proscribed place, off limits because now it is forbidden by men.

LAUNCESTON JAIL

One of two jails (the other being Bodmin) where women accused of witchcraft were sent and often held for long periods before being brought to trial (see Witchcraft In Cornwall). Many women committed to jails of this type subsequently died because of the appalling conditions that prevailed. James Nield, writing in 1812, describes Launceston jail as being "in a most filthy and dilapidated state." There was no water, no privy and no courtyard "in which the prisoners might take exercise." In some rooms the doors were only four feet high and fifteen inches wide. In others the light came from an aperture measuring three feet by nine inches and that light was almost obscured by an iron bar. "Straw lay scattered about the floor, and there was a fireplace - but no fuel allowed." Bodmin jail was a little better according to a writer reporting in 1799. Even so, the women prisoners were herded together cheek by jowl in one room.

LOGAN STONE

According to Hunt, the Logan stone near Lands End was a midnight rendezvous for witches. They assembled at these meetings having flown on stems of ragwort to Castle Peak on moonlit nights. It was also the gathering place of many witches who left for Wales where they would drink the milk of the Welsh cows. From Logan's rock witches would also sit and watch ships come to grief, having raised a tempest.

MADGY FIGGY

The most famous, and possibly infamous of Cornwall's witches, immortalised in the audio-visual presentation at The Lands End Complex by a stereotypical hag. Madge (or Madgy) Figgy is not mentioned prior to Robert Hunt (1881). According to his account, this most celebrated of the St Levan and St Buryan witches was in the habit of sitting on the "Chair Ladder", a pile of granite boulders near St Levan, where she would command the storms and lure ships to the rocks. She also headed bands of witches who would fly on their ragwort stems to Spain and Wales. Madge lived in a cottage not far from Raftra. Once, in a storm, a Portugese ship was shipwrecked. Among the bodies found on the shore was that of a richly attired woman. Though the body was stripped by wreckers, Madge demanded her treasures should be returned. At night local people would see a strange light pass from the place where the unknown woman had been buried into Madge's hut at Tol Pedden. This continued for three months. Then a stranger arrived who did not speak English. He asked to be shown the woman's grave. He sat there until nightfall, when he then followed the light to Madge's hut and found there the woman's treasure. He rewarded the wreckers and then left. Madge's comment was: One witch knows another witch, dead or living.The African would have been the death of us if we hadn't kept the treasure

MAZE, SPIRAL

The maze is oneof the universal symbols of the goddess and was used by Celtic peoples. Carvings of mazes are to be found carved on rocks, especially in Ireland. In Cornwall there are three well preserved examples of rock carvings of this kind. Two are to be found in Rocky Valley, near Bossiney, North Cornwall. The third is to be seen in the Witchcraft Museum, Boscastle. The Rocky Valley mazes are described as being "Bronze Age" according to the adjacent sign but it seems likely that they are not quite as ancient as this since they are not particularly weathered. The valley is associated with the 6th Century Saint Nectan and it is possible that they may have been carved there at this period .

The carving is on a piece of blue slate measuring 18 inches. A label attached to the stone says that it originates from a farm near Michaelstow, a village south of Boscastle. The owner of the museum, Cecil Williamson, says that the stone was donated to the museum in 1950 by the daughter of a Manx wisewoman (witch) called Kate the Gull. According to Mr Williamson, the stone originally came from "across the water" (see "The Riddle of The Mazes", J & D Saward, Meyn Mamvro, Issue 5). Shortly after the museum opened in 1958, Mr Williamson was told by a local wise woman that her mother once had a stone similar to the one in the museum. The stones were once known as "Troy stones" in the south west and were used for magical purposes. The witch/ wise woman would induce a state of trance by tracing her finger over the shape of the maze. This would be accompanied by ritual humming. They were also known as "brain stones" and moonstones, especially when worked at night. During the day time the stones were kept wrapped in a cloth.

MAY

An important month in the tradition of witchcraft and still important, despite attempts by government to eliminate May Day from the British calendar. (Similar attempts were made by the Puritans during the period of the Commonwealth but to no avail. One Puritan writer described the maypole as "that stinking idol".)

Cornwall is renowned for being a county which eschewed Puritan tradition and it has kept the old customs alive down the centuries. The OBBY OSS ceremony is the most well known example of this living pagan tradition. (see OBBY OSS) At one time not only May Day itself but also the first Sunday of May (the Christian Sabbath !) was put aside for ritual celebration and parties of three or four families would travel to neighbouring villages for picnics. Maypoles were common right up until the middle of the nineteenth century in Cornwall. Villages would vie to capture each others maypoles (OCS Vol 12, 2-3) and sometimes they would deliberately vandalise them. This was known as "The challenge of the Maypole". This custom was common in St Neot. In West Cornwall it was customary for boys to fix may boughs over a farmer's door before he was up in the morning. The farmer was then obliged to give the boys their breakfast. Horns and whistles were blown, especially in the town of St Ives, in order to drive away evil spirits. In Helston and Padstow, even today, green boughs are collected and placed over doorways of houses so that the spirit of the forest was seen to protect the inhabitants. In Penzance, according to Hunt,, it was the custom for young people to sit up until 12 o'clock and then march round the town playing violins and pipes to summon their friends to the Maying. When all were assembled, they went into the country and visited farmhouses where they were supplied with rum and milk. They then gathered the "May" or branches and leaves of young trees. In Polperro, children and adults went and collected elm or white thorn. At a later hour boys would venture forth with buckets and "dip" or nearly drown anyone they saw who was not carrying a piece of may blossom. At East and West Looe, boys dressed their hats with flowers and carried bullocks' horns in which sticks two feet long were fixed. These were filled with water and used to assault any person they saw not carrying the May. (Also see FLORA DAY)

Midsummer is one of the great eight Celtic festivals and celebrated by followers of the Old Religion. In Cornwall, as in many other counties, it is a time often associated with fertility and sexual congress. Several customs commerorate this fact. According to Hunt, if on midsummer eve a young woman takes off her shift and, having washed it, turns it inside out, hanging it on the back of a chair near the fire, she will see, around midnight, her future husband who comes and turns the shift for her. Also if a young woman walks backwards into her garden on midsummer eve and plucks a rose there, she will know the identity of her future husband. The rose has to be sewn up in a paper bag and put aside in a drawer and remain there until Christmas Day.

Hemp seed was also sown on midsummer eve by young women, to the words:

"Hemp seed I sow,
Hemp seed I hoe
And he
Who my true love will be
Come after me and mow."

An apparation of the lover would then appear. Courtney recalls how "maidens" would rise early on midsumer's eve and go into the country in search of an even leafed ash or clover. When found, they would repeat love charms. According to Hunt, all the witches in West Cornwall used to meet on this night at Trewa in Zennor and around the dying fires "renew their vows to their master, the Devil." Hunt was of course, a traditionalist in his misrepresentation of the Old Religion. The Devil was not known to witches and was a fiction used for political reasons by the Church, especially in its legislative arm of the Inquisition when condemning and torturing witches in Western Europe..

Mother Louse, the traditional conception of a witch. From Caulfield's Wonderful Museum of Remarkable Portraits, London 1794.

The pellar (see PELLAR) or white witch (see WITCH) in Cornwall often used a magical ring made from blue stone or glass called the MILPREVE. It is mentioned as long ago as Carew (survey of Cornwall, 1602) who says: " The countrey people retaine a conceite that the snakes by their breathing about a hazel wand doe make a stone ring of blew colour in which there appeareth the yellow figure of a snake, and that the beasts which are stung, being given to drink of the water wherein this stone hath been soaked, will there through recover."

Hunt, writing in 1881 (Romances of the West of England), remarks that adders once swarmed around Lands End and conjectures that the MILPREVES may have been balls of coraline lime stone. He refers to the stones as "Druidic rings". In a letter written in 1701 to the author, Lhuys gives an account of the superstitions relating to MILPREVES. "The Cornish retain a variety of charms, and have still towards the Land's End the amulets of Maen Magal and Glain - Neider, which latter they call a Melprer, a thousand worms, and have a charm for the snake to make it, when they have found one asleep, and struck a hazel-wand in the centre of its spirae."

The name MILPREVE is from the Cornish MYLPREF - a thousand snakes. It was thought to be an unfailing remedy against snake bite to carry one of these. Snake stones or adder stones occur elsewhere in folklore, but especially in Scotland where they were once called Adder stane. They were found frequently in the 19th Century in Bronze Age barrows and were deposited with the ashes of the dead. Jo O'Cleirigh, writing in Meyn Mamvro No. 1, mentions the fact that one of the names for the druids was Nadredd or "Adders". Among the Welsh and the Irish, Druidical beads were called Gleim na Droedh or Glaine nan Druidhe, meaning the magician's glass. A MILPREVE can be found in the Penzance Museum at Penlee House. Bottrell refers to this as the Clain Neider or Adders Bead and says that the stone was found at the Boscawen Un Stone Circle. There is a long tradition of these stones in Cornwall dating from the late Bronze Age.

The healing properties of the MILPREVES were attested to by the Rev. Malan, writing in the late 19th Century (Notes on the Neighbourhood of Brown Willy) who notes that he had been shown a MILPREVE which had been in a family for generations and that it was valued very highly. It was especially used as a cure for bad eye conditions and the user would strike the bad eye each morning with the MILPREVE.

Stones sacred to the goddess of the Old Religion are most likely to have been used by witches. German Aryan tradition said that a serpent with a magic stone in its head would be found at the root of every hazel tree (witchwood) and the serpent's stone was sacred to the moon. Hazel was regarded by the Celts as the tree of wisdom and of healing. It was also associated with divination. The serpent's stone was also associated with the Philosopher's stone which would bring eternal life. Remnants of the serpent's phallic symbolism appeared in medieval charms such as the belief that "female diseases" could be got rid of by applying to the sufferer a staff which had been used to beat a snake. In fact immortality was the special province of the skin-shedding serpent and the Goddess from very early times. Ancient people believed that since the snake shed its skin it was capable of perpetual renewal.

MOON CUSTOMS AND SUPERSTITIONS

The moon was sacred to Hecate and Diana, long regarded as the forms of the goddess sacred to witches. In Cornwall, moon customs and superstitions were once rife. Seeing the new moon in the old moon's arms was regarded as a sign of a change in the weather. Herbs for drying were traditionally gathered at full moon and winter fruit was picked and stored at the full moon so as not to lose its plumpness. Timber had to be felled on the waning of the moon because the sap was then down and the wood more durable. (Courtney) To see the new moon for the first time through glass was thought to be unlucky for it was certain that the glass would break before the moon was out. People would also go out of doors when they saw a new moon in order to give her a votive offering, usually a piece of gold or money. (Hunt) It was thought advisable to cut your hair by the growing moon and if it was on the wane, baldness would surely follow. The men of Gorran attempted to trap the moon's reflection in a bucket and throw it over a cliff, having decided that it was entirely responsible for the bad weather. In fact the moon was seen as a weather prophet, as proved by the old saying:

A fog and a small moon
Bring an easterly wind soon.

OATES, WILLIAM

A pellar and herbalist, famous throughout Cornwall and better known as "Jimmy the Witch". William Rapson Oates had commenced his career in 1868 but spent many years in prison because of his criminal activities. From the outset he described himself as one who was regularly engaged by farmers in Devon and Cornwall to protect their cattle against witchcraft. He was indicted on 29 January 1894 for pretending to exercise witchcraft and sorcery (West Briton Newspaper). On 29th December he had informed Mary Sedgman that her daughter, who was greatly ill, was under a spell and that he could find out who had cast it. He also claimed that he was a Dr Thomas and a brother of the famous wizard of that name from St Austell. He also claimed to have cured a cow belonging to Sedgman and was accused of borrowing money from her. He was charged much later (in September, 1894) with vagrancy at Helston Magistrates Court and sent to prison for a fortnight.

OBBY OSS

The Obby Oss ceremony is Cornwall's oldest pagan festival and is performed on May Day in Padstow. It is the only European pagan festival which has survived in its present form unchristianized for at least 800 years. Although the origins of the Obby Oss are shrouded in obscurity, there are several indications that this is a Celtic festival of great antiquity, designed to promote fertility.

The term "Obby Oss" has been interpreted as Hobby Horse and there are, of course Hobby Horses in Wales (the Mari Lwyd), Minehead, Somerset and Kent. The horse was regarded as a sacred creature by the Celts and the goddess Epona, a horse goddess, is still remembered in the great chalk hill figure at Uffington, Oxfordshire. The word Oss in Old English actually means "God", however, and it is interesting that of all the ."Horses", the Oss least resembles a horse. The dress is made of black sailcloth, and the head is a fierce mask with red eyes. It also comprises a horse's mane and there is a tail distended by a hoop. In addition it has a tall pointed cap and oak snappers. The jaws are studded with nails to represent teeth. On the front of the cap appear the letters O B. In front of the Oss dances the teazer or dancer who carries a club. The dancers emerge from the Golden Lion pub at 10 am on May Day and proceed up and down the streets of Padstow until the evening. The song itself has parallels to the Hal An Tow at Helston and evokes the energy and fertility of May Day. At one point the Oss dies and has to be revived in a manner similar to St George and the Dragon in the mumming play.

Tradition tells of an attempted French invasion of Pastow during the siege of Calais between 1346 - 7. The mythical figure of "Aunt Ursula Birdhood" saved the town by getting the women of Padstow to dress in red cloaks and dance on Stepper Point with the Oss. The French saw this spectacle and fled in horror. There may be some substance in this for until 1850 the Oss was accompanied by an old woman in a scarlet cloak There is a clue here that the dance may once have been a women's dance and the Old Woman figure might have been the Crone or Priestess.

There is no doubt that the Oss ceremony is a survival of an original Celtic festival. The dance itself has a peculiar hypnotic ring which produces in the spectators and participants a trace state. The actual dance of the Oss and the teaser is a spiral dance - one of the most ancient forms of dance known to humanity and similar in form to dances still performed in Africa by women's groups. In fact there is some similarity between the Oss and a mask assumed by dancers in New Guinea. If anyone were in doubt about the power to evoke fertility produced by the dance they should recall the tradition that it is good luck for a woman to touch the skirts of the Oss and should she disappear under the skirts of the Oss, then her fertility may be assured. That the Obby Oss ceremony has survived at all is remarkable and may be to do with Padstow's isolated position and the strong family links that pertain to the town. It is the most significant links we have with the rituals of the Old Religion.

THE PELLER

The peller (usually called pellar) was the name given to those inheritors of the witchcraft tradition who were renowned for their abilities as healers and divinators. The native tradtion which had been inherited from the 17th Century had long since been suppressed. By the mid 1600's the legislation enacted under the King James statute (known as the Witchcraft Act) had led to a widespread condemnation of the old craft among women, who had been largely marginalised as either white witches, black witches or midwives. In Cornwall large numbers of women had been brought to trial during the 17th Century, mainly on trumped up charges and the squirearchy kept a careful eye on those who advertised their talents in the areas of healing and divination.

As a unified tradition witchcraft had not survived intact. It had been split into distinct areas of craft: Conjurors (including astrologers), charmers and Cunning men or women. In Cornwall, however, the Conjurors or pellars were the most powerful of them all.

The reputation of the pellar survived until late into the 19th Century and was commented upon by newspapers and folklorists alike. The name itself is obscure. Craig Weatherhill (Myths and Legends of Cornwall) believes that the word is a corruption of "expeller" - i.e. an expeller of spells..

The pellars (sometimes spelt pellers) were thought to be a descendant of one Matthew Lutey, an inhabitant of Cury, on the lizard. Lutey's story is told in full in my Witchcraft In Cornwall. Briefly, Lutey assisted a mermaid and prevented her from being stranded by the incoming tide. In return he was given three gifts: the ability to break spells, to charm illnesses away and to find stolen goods. As part of the contract Lutey loses his own life. The significance of the three gifts is obvious: three is the number of the goddess and the concept of the male use of the mermaid's gifts entails a necessary propitiation.

One of the most famous of the pellars was Tamsin Blight (alias Tammy Blee) of Helston. Even today her reputation in Helston is renowned among older Cornish folk. Tamsin came from Redruth. She left her husband, James Thomas and soon carved out a reputation for herself as a powerfull pellar in the Helston area. It is significant that she retained her maiden name, a practice followed especially by women who were practitioners of the old craft where matrilinal descent was valued. According to local tradition, Tamsin became aware of her powers when quite young. By the time she was aged it was not unknown for people to arrive at her house on stretchers and for them to leave unassisted (weatherhill & Devereaux). According to Bottrell, "The conjurer received the people and their offering singly, in the room by courtesy styled the "hale" (hall). Few remained closeted with him for more than half an hour, during which time some were provided with little bags of earth, teeth or bones taken from a grave. These precious relics were to be worn suspended from the neck, for the cure or prevention of fits, and other mysterious complaints brought on by witchcraft." Others were given a piece of parchment on which was written a charm. People were also given witch powders. Others were provided with milpreves or snake stones. (See

MILPREVES)

According to Courtney (Cornish Feasts And Folklore), the charms given by a pellar were wrapped in velvet or parchment and on the outside an inscription was written such as: "By the help of the Lord these will do good." The use of Christian prayers or utterances in pagan spells or charms goes back some way as is evidenced by the Anglo Saxon Leech books.

Another charm given by pellars was the "kinning stones". These were amulets given for ailments of the eye. According to a clergyman from North Cornwall (Rev. A. H. Malan, Notes on the neighbourhood of Brown Willy) the stones were "translucent, blueish-white globular crystal, about one and a quarter inch in diameter; in texture horny rather than vitreous; apparently not made of glass, but perhaps of rock crystal... This kind of amulet is worn around the neck."

The reports of pellars and their work follow throughout the mid 19th Century. Despite the onslaught of Wesleyan Methodism, with its emphasis on hellfire and the Devil as a real entity representing pagan tradition, the folk tradition still believed in the efficacy of the pellar.

Weatherhill and Devereaux mention a powerful pellar who lived near the Tamar in Plymouth who was often called across into Cornwall. He visited both Tintagel, where a farmer's cattle had died and another farmer in St Ewe who had a child afflicted with eye disease. The West Briton newspaper for 28 October 1836 reports the fact that the man had lost all faith with conventional medicine. The report goes on to record:

"The witch came ... by coach, and soon after refreshment, all the paraphernalia of the occult science were put into operation; and in a few days the important matter was brought to a crisis. She could not counteract what the black witch had done, but she had put to a stop all future influence, and moreover gave the parents a clear idea who was the author of the child's illness.... Many believe that the witch, in her journey from Plymouth, raised the late severe storm, for it was observed that, on the road as she came, houses were unroofed, and trees torn up by their roots."

In September 1844 another pellar from Helston (not Tamsin Blight) is recorded as having carried out elaborate rituals at Phillack churchyard, Hayle. According to the report, several people afflicted,with a disease "engaged a scatterer of witch spells from Helston, to whom they disclosed every incident of their own lives". Having gone to the churchyard with the pellar, the company watched as he "walked many times around the church, the doors and windows opened and shut at his bidding. Then he commanded them to remain open, and as they were passed in succession, he brought the persons who had ill-wished to their face."

So common and widespread was the power and reputation of the pellar that the West Briton voiced the view (2 May 1856) that "vast numbers of people" were credulous enough to believe in their powers. "it used to be Johhny Hooper of Ladock; it is now Mr --- Thomas of Nanstallan, in the parish of Bodmin. This man carries on a flourishing trade in the conjuring way and seldom goes home from a fair or market quite sober, and withal is an immoderate snuff-taker."

The popularity and success of the pellar in Cornish society demonstrates to what extent the Old Religion had resisted the onslaught of the "Official" religion. It was the last survival of the healing arts which had been wrested from the traditional witch as a result of four hundred years of continued persecution.

The Transvection of Witches (shapeshifting), from The Werewolf, Montague Summers.

PENTREATH, DOLLY

Dolly Pentreath was supposed to be the last person to speak Cornish in Cornwall. She died in 1777 and was buried in Paul churchyard. According to Bottrell, she was a follower of the Old Religion, being expert in fortune telling, charming cures for diseases and giving directions to young people regarding the choice of a love partner. She was expert in magic, both creative and destructive and was a powerful layer of spells.

SNAKES

Snakes or serpents were from ancient times associated with the goddess, as in the statue of Diana of Ephesus, who holds serpents in either hand. In Cornwall a number of superstitions connected with the sacredness of serpents persisted. The Milpreve stone for example was otherwise known as "a thousand worms" (see MILPREVE). It was believed that these scrying stones were made by a snake which would be enchanted once asleep by the act of striking a hazel wand at the centre of its spirae. It was also said that no kind of snake was ever to be found near the ash tree and that a branch of the ash tree would prevent a snake from coming near a person. (Hunt). The sacred quality of the snake, in concurrence with the beliefs of the Old Religion, is demonstrated by a story which Hunt tells. A child was in the habit of receiving its portion of bread and milk at the cottage door and sharing it with an adder who was a close friend. The mother of the child found this out and bound an ash twig round its body to protect it when she was out working. The adder no longer came near the child but from that day forward the child pined and eventually died for the loss of his friend. This story illustrates well the Celtic belief of the totem animal or "fetch" which was the child's friend. It is interesting to note that Hunt also mentions a charm to drive away snakes. A circle is drawn round the snake and a Christian psalm (the 68th) repeated. The ability to drive away snakes was often designated to Christian saints , especially St Patrick, who rid Ireland of these creatures.

STONE CIRCLES

Stone circles in Cornwall were traditionally connected with practitioners of the Old Religion and their folklore reflects this. The circles are thought to belong to the neolithic period and were no doubt venerated from that period. There is sufficient evidence to suggest that such sites were linked to a Goddess based religion.

Several circles in Cornwall are given the names "Nine Maidens" or "Merry Maidens" and the number nine is significant in terms of the goddess since it a combination of three, her sacred number (Maiden, Mother and Crone). The Nine Maidens was the name given to a group of young women who broke the Sabbath Law against dancing and were therefore turned into stone by an avenging God. The concept of women dancing as a threat to Christianity thus suggests the continued power held by women well into the medieval period in Cornwall. The Hurlers, a group of stones near Liskeard, were also turned to stone for hurling (throwing a metal ball to each other) for the same reason. There are also Nine Maidens near Wendron (Stithian/ Helston area) where a similar legend applies, although here the stones mark the graves of nine sisters (according to Hunt) who have been similarly metamorphosed.

There are other neolithic sites which carry connections with Cornish witchcraft legends. These include Crows an Wra, between Penzance and Lands End. This means "The Witch's cross" or more exactly "the cross of the Hag/Crone". At Lewannick is "Joan's Pitcher", a holy well recalling a female guardian. Near Zennor a rock formation called Witch's Rock was thought to have been an important site for local Midsummer Eve celebrations by followers of the Craft. At Lands End a chair shaped rock was thought to have been occupied by the legendary siren witch, Madgy Figgy.

THOMAS, MARTIN

A pellar and witch who lived at Redruth in the 1840's (Hunt), Thomas Martin was renowned for his soothsaying ability, and his ability to cure children of fits and deformities by means of charms. A woman once made an appointment to meet Thomas at a certain stile in order to have her fortune told. She went to the appointed stile only to be met with by a large black snake. As Thomas did not appear she assumed that the soothsayer had shapeshifted into the snake. She decided then and there not to consult him further, now fearing his power.

Bewitched woman and suitor, from A Certain relation of the Hog-Faced Gentlewoman, 1640.

ANNA TRAPNELL.

In 1654 Anna Trapnel published four texts. One of these, entitled "Anna Trapnel's Report And Plea", described her journey from London into Cornwall and her "proclaiming the rage and strivings of the people against the comings forth of the Lord Jesus to reign, manifested in the harsh, rough, boisterous, rugged, inhumane and uncivil usage of Anna Trapnel by the justices and people in Cornwall, at a place called Truro."

In April 1653 the Rump Parliament had been dissolved and in July Cromwell had called together a new assembly of men who came to be known as the Barebones Parliament. Among the 140 members were a dozen Fifth Monarchists and other radicals and these elements began to push for reforms of the tithe system and the law. However, by December, power had returned to the army and for the Fifth Monarchists this was a betrayal. This was the political background, then, to Anna's trip to Cornwall.

In January 1654 Anna attended a meeting held in Whitehall, London, by Vavasor Powell, a Baptist and Fifth Monarchist preacher and it was here that she fell into a trance which lasted twelve days. During this time her friends recorded many of her prophetic prayers and utterances. By February friends of Cromwell had noted Anna as a possible trouble maker. They were not wrong. Anna published two tracts: "The Cry of A Stone" and "Strange And Wonderful News From Whitehall", and then travelled to Cornwall where she had friends. By March she had been arrested. In Truro she had fallen into a trance once more whilst staying at the house of Captain Langdon and by now her fame had spread so that many people visited her out of curiosity, "some out of good will and others to gaze". In Anna's "Report And Plea", she describes how "the clergymen and the jurors (contrived) an indictment against me". In fact a Mr Welstead called for her arrest, claiming that she was "an imposter, and a dangerous deceiver". Trapnel's prophetic trances were in fact used against her on the grounds that she was guilty of witchcraft. This was by no means a unique occurrence. The same thing happened to Anne Jefferies of St Teath, a monarchist and most probably a defender of the use of the traditional prayer book (although in Anne's case she claimed to have had concourse with the faery folk and to have been supplied food by them. This would give the authorities much greater grounds for accusing her of witchcraft as in the 17th Century there was in the folk consciousness a clear link between the belief in the "fey folk" and witchcraft. In fact Anne had been arrested in the same year and had also come under the scrutiny of Justice Tregagle of Trevorder, a man who was determined to root out women who might prove troublesome to the establishment.

Anna's account of her arrest and condemnation as a witch is quite dramatic. She desribes how "These justices that came to fetch me out of my bed, they made a great tumult, thenm and their followers in the house, and some came upstairs crying "A witch ! A witch !", making a great stir on the stairs. And a poor honest man rebuking such that said so, he was tumbled downstairs and beaten too, by one of the justice's followers. And the justices made a great noise in putting out of my chamber where I lay many of my friends; and they said if my friends would not take me up, they would have some should take me up. One of my friends told them that they must fetch their silk gowns to do it then, for the poor would not do it. And they threatened much but the Lord overruled them."

Anna was then physically abused by her tormentors but she refused to budge. A witch trier was then called but apparently did not materialise, a fact which Anna saw as a form of divine intervention. The authorities then tried to get up a bill of indictment against Captain Langdon, her friend, but without success. Two women, who had promised to bear witness against Anna, subsequently withdrew their testimony on the advice of friends

When Anna was finally forced to attend the sessions house she faced her accusers stolidly. "I espied a clergyman at their (the justices') elbow, who helped to make their indictment (and) though he and the witch trying woman looked steadfastly in my face, it did no way dismay me, nor the grim fierce looks of the justices did not daunt me, for as soon as I beheld them I remembered a dear friend to Christ". There then follows a detailed account of the trial proceedings during which Anna showed considerable skill and ability in sidestepping accusations about uttering false prophecies and seditious claims. When the two witnesses for the prosecution failed to materialise, the case against her weakened, but she was bound over to be of good behaviour and asked to commit a regognizance of £300 - a large sum of money in those days. This was a surety or bond to ensure that she would be of good behaviour. Captain Langdon and her friend Major Bawden (also a Fifth Monarchist) each pledged £150 on her behalf, a sign of their commitment to her cause. Anna concludes her account by saying: "And as I went in the crowd, many strangers were very loving and careful to help me out of the crowd; and the rude multitude said, "Sure this woman is no witch, for she speaks many good words, which the witches could not." And thus the Lord made the rude rabble to justify his appearance. For in all that was said by me, I was nothing, the Lord put all in my mouth, and toild me what I should say..."

Anna's case is a fascinating one, especially when compared to that of Anne Jefferies. Unlike Anne, she got off lightly and was not imprisoned for her utterances. Tregagle called Anna a "dreamer" and at the conclusion of the trial told her to "Take no care for us". Clearly he did not see her as a genuine threat. Or was it that the justices feared the strength of opinion of the rabble in Truro who had turned out to cheer and support her ? We shall never know. However, Anna's detailed account of her trial and the accusations against her are one of the clearest depictions we have of how the term "witch" was used as a portmanteau idea in order to condemn those outspoken women in 17th Century Cornwall who dared to challenge the establishment view.

WELLS, HOLY

The holy wells of Cornwall all bear the names of Christian Saints. Yet before Christianity claimed them for its own, they marked the places where sacred water flowed from the body of the Earth Mother and as such they were venerated by followers of the Old Religion. Wells were certainly sacred to the Celtic people who once populated Cornwall. Their folklore is legion. Perhaps the most famous of all is Madron Well, near Penzance. Here miraculous cures for ailments were recorded as long ago as the 15th Century. Madron had its own tradition of guardians, all of whom were women. In West Cornwall children were taken before sunrise in May to the holy wells to be dipped in the running water and were plunged three times in the waters of the wells, the parents facing the sun and passing round the wells nine times from east to west. Small pieces of clothing torn from the body of a person (called clooties) were tied to the branches of overhanging thorns or may trees as a propitiation of the goddess and to mark which ailment the person suffered from. Love divination was also practised by young girls, especially in May by the dropping of pins or small pieces of straw into the waters of the well. To Figgy Dowdy's Well on Carn Martha Hill, near Redruth it was a tradition until the 1930's for children to take their dolls on Good Friday, in order to have them "baptized". This is no doubt a corruption of the pagan tradition of the offering of "harvest dolls".

The healing properties of the wells varied. For example, Chapel Farm well at St Breward was considered good for sore eyes. St Nun's Well at Atlarnon cured insanity. The beautiful little well in Buryan, St Alsia, and St Piran's in Perranzabuloe, were good for rickets. Jesus Well in St Minver was reputed to cure whooping cough. The waters of St Uny's Well, Redruth, were said to prevent a baptized person from being hanged. St Martin's well at Liskeard was known for its beneficial influence on married life.

WITCHES, WHITE AND BLACK

The distinction between a white and a black witch is entirely erroneous and reflects the perception of the witch developed and encouraged by the Christian church in its suppression of pagan practices. In early times the concept of the "wise woman" or witch (the name means: one who bends or turns and is Anglo Saxon in origin) was commonly upheld by folk belief. As the Christian authorities began to persecute paganism, however, witches were then seen in an unfavourable light as those who might seek to do harm to others. These were "black witches". Those who sought to remove curses or spells were "white witches" and it is interesting to note that they were often men. In fact the concept of doing harm to others is not part of the European witchcraft tradition, despite the immense propaganda disseminated by the Inquisition of the Medieval period and is entirely an invention of their paranoia. White witches in Cornwall were known as "pellars". It is significant that in all the surviving folklore so called "black witches" are all mythical figures (see MADGY FIGGY) whom men feared because of their ability to curse and command the forces of nature. It was of course the fear of women, their traditions and power that gave rise to their persecution in Cornwall as in many other counties during the period of the European witch hunts.

HANNAH TRAPNEL,

A Quaker and pretended Prophetess

(From a scarce Print by Gaywood)

A SELECT BIBLIOGRAPHY

The literature relating to Cornish witchcraft is, to put it mildly, disappointing. Cornish folklore per se is well represented by such mid to late nineteenth century authors as William Bottrell and Robert Hunt, the latter owing much to the former and therefore considerably more literary in style. Margaret Courtney (Cornish Feasts And Folklore, Oakmagic Publications, 1998) was a reliable folkorist, collecting much of her material from local clergymen and people in the Penwith area. Further afield, C. Hammond (another priest !) is reliable for the St Austell area and so too was Jonathan Couch, a doctor from Polperro (Customs & Superstitions Of East Cornwall, Oakmagic Publications, 1998). Another well informed folklorist was T. Thiselton -Dyer, whose English Folkore should certainly be consulted. Hamilton-Jenkin, the Cornish writer and bard, collected some interesting secondhand accounts of witchcraft in his Cornwall And Its People. For a detailed examination of the Anne Jefferies case one should certainly read Moses Pitt's account, reprinted in Anne Jefferies And The Fairies (Oakmagic Publications, 1996) and also the very illuminating biography of Tregeagle in Barbara Spooner's John Tregagle of Trevorder: Man And Ghost, Truro, 1935. Apart from newspapers such as the West Briton, The Cornishman and The Western Morning News, those interested in wider research may also wish to consult the extensive volumes of the Old Cornwall Society and also, to a lesser extent, Devon & Cornwall Notes & Queries. For a brief survey of witchcraft in Cornwall, the author's Witchcraft In Cornwall (Oakmagic Publications, 1995) is worth looking at as is the thesis by Christine Corey, "Possession And Persecution...", although sadly this useful investigation into religious intolerance in 17th century Cornwall is only available as a single reference volume at Launceston Public Library. Hopefully, one day it may be published for wider enjoyment. Certainly the reader would wish to consult Ewen L'Estrange's Witchcraft & Demoniasm, 1933, for a full account of the pamphlet literature and gaol book records for the county, although again this is long out of print. Reference has been made in the text of the invaluable Museum of Witchcraft, located at Boscastle, N. Cornwall. The museum not only has an extensive collection of artefacts (accessible through the internet) but has also recently acquired extra items from Cecil Williamson's vast collection. There is also a comprehensive library at the museum, accessible strictly by appointment with the curator, Graham King.